PACIFIC SEA SHELLS

PACIFIC SEA SHELLS

A HANDBOOK OF COMMON MARINE MOLLUSCS
OF
HAWAII AND THE SOUTH SEAS

(REVISED EDITION)

By

SPENCER WILKIE TINKER
Director of the Aquarium
University of Hawaii

CHARLES E. TUTTLE COMPANY : PUBLISHERS
Rutland, Vermont & Tokyo, Japan

To My Parents

Luke Tinker and Anna V. Overholser Tinker

Published by the Charles E. Tuttle Company
of Rutland, Vermont & Tokyo, Japan
with editorial offices at 15 Edogawa-cho
Bunkyo-ku, Tokyo, Japan

All rights reserved
Library of Congress Catalog Card No. 57-13069
First edition, 1952
Second edition, revised, 1958
Third printing, 1960

Printed in Japan

PREFACE

This volume was prepared to serve as a handbook for amateur shell collectors who are interested in Pacific Ocean shells. It is written to help and to encourage the student and the beginner in the identification of the more common and larger central Pacific species.

This book is not a complete guide to all of the sea shells of the Pacific Ocean. It is primarily a guide to the larger and more common shells of the Hawaiian Islands and of the area lying to the south and to the west of this group. Because nearly all of the Hawaiian species are found over wide areas in the Pacific Ocean, it is hoped that this little book will prove to be very useful to amateur collectors in all of the areas of the tropical Pacific Ocean.

The many minute species and the rare and uncommon species are not included within this volume because they are either difficult to obtain or to study and are therefore not often found in the collections of amateurs.

Of the five classes of molluscs, the snail-like forms or gastropods comprise the major portion of this book because they are the most interesting, the most numerous, and the most often found in shell collections.

The arrangement of the families of shells in this book follows the *Check List and Bibliography of the Recent Marine Molluscs of Japan* by Tokubei Kuroda and Tadashige Habe. The species listed follow in part an unpublished check list of Hawaiian molluscs prepared by E. H. Bryan, Jr. of Honolulu.

The author is pleased to acknowledge the assistance and council of the individuals who helped in the preparation of this book.

Dr. C. M. Burgess of Honolulu made his collection available for the project and it is from this remarkable collection that most of the photographs have been taken. The author owes a debt of gratitude to Dr. Burgess for his generosity and help in this project.

The author also wishes to express his appreciation to Dr. James W. Cherry, Mr. Wray Harris, Mr. Jens M. Ostergaard, Mr. James Pang, Mr. Ditlev Thaanum and Mr. Kenneth A. Wong all of Honolulu, Hawaii, for their help in the preparation of this book.

SPENCER TINKER

Honolulu, Hawaii

TABLE OF CONTENTS

INTRODUCTION

The molluscs are a large group of more than 60,000 species and are, next to the insects, the largest assemblage of animals in point of numbers on the face of the earth.

These creatures, although they differ among themselves, have certain characteristics which separate them from all other animals and at the same time unite them into a fairly well defined group. These characters, although a little difficult for beginners, should be mentioned here.

Molluscs are what zoologists call triploblastic animals. This means that as molluscs develop from their egg they produce three kinds of cells or germ layers from which their bodies are subsequently developed.

Molluscs also are bilaterally symmetrical in shape and have their bodies divided into a right and a left side which are approximately the same. Likewise they are not divided into segments as are the insects and many of the worms, but have a body which extends from front to back without any interruptions or crosswise partitions.

Molluscs possess a characteristic structure called a foot. It is a large muscular organ on the under side of the body and is used by many of them as a means of locomotion. They also possess an alimentary tract with a mouth and an anus and have, in addition, a space within their body called a coelom into which their internal organs project somewhat the same as ours do.

Another feature of this group, and the one in which we are most interested, is the shell. Nearly all molluscs have a shell at some time during their life history and in some of these creatures the shell may be very large, interesting, and beautiful.

This large group or phylum of the molluscs is further divided by scientists into five smaller groups or classes, the members of which look still more alike because they are more closely related to each other. These five classes are mentioned below.

The first class, the chitons and their relatives, is called Amphineura, meaning double nerve because of the manner in which their nervous system is organized. They are slug-like creatures, most of which have eight plates imbedded in their upper side. In numbers, they are a small group and are not particularly interesting to shell collectors.

The second class, the snails, slugs and their relatives, is called Gastropoda, a word which means stomach-footed. They have a broad flat

9

foot on which they slide along and have in addition an asymmetrical body. Most of the members of this group have a spirally coiled shell, although it may be small or even absent in some of the forms. It is the shells of this group which comprise the major portion of this book.

The third class, the tooth or tusk shells, is called Scaphopoda, a word which means boot-footed. They all make their home within a shell which is tubular in shape and open at both ends like the truncated tusk of an elephant.

The fourth class, the bivalves, is called Pelecypoda, a word which means hatchet-footed. This group includes the clams, mussels, oysters, and scallops. They all possess a paired shell which permits their ready identification as members of this class. This group is not included in this volume.

The fifth class, the Cephalopoda or head-footed molluscs, includes the octopods, the squids, and the nautiloids. Although they do not closely resemble the other molluscs, they are nevertheless related to them. The shells of the nautiloids are very beautiful and are often found in shell collections.

Of these five groups or classes of molluscs, the gastropods make up the greater part of this volume. These gastropods, as well as the other classes of molluscs, are further divided into smaller groups called "orders" and these orders are still further divided into smaller groups called "families." It is these family groups with which the shell collector must first become familiar. It is the pattern of this book to present the common gastropods by families in such a manner that the members of a particular family will be found upon the same page or at least upon adjacent pages. This will permit the student or collector to compare his specimen with the other members of the group to which it belongs and also to form a mental picture of the general types of shells which are within each family group.

THE SNAIL-LIKE MOLLUSCS

CLASS GASTROPODA

Of the five great groups or classes of molluscs, the gastropods or snail-like molluscs are by far the largest group. Within this group are many thousands of species which were so widely distributed in ancient times that today they may be found in almost every corner of the earth.

Not only are these molluscs widely distributed over the earth, but they have adjusted themselves to a wide variety of living conditions. They have accustomed themselves to habitats ranging from the freezing cold near the polar regions to the intense heat of the tropics and from life beneath the sea to land so dry as to scarcely support life. Wherever they dwell, whether it be in the tops of lofty trees, over the vast stretches of the land, through the lakes and rivers, along the shoreline, far out over the surface of the sea, or even down into the abyssal darkness of the ocean, each place has become the chosen home for some group of molluscs.

The animals included within this group of snail-like molluscs are a diverse lot and very widely in their size, body structure, shells, habits, and in their general mode of life. They include a range of forms varying in size from animals so small as to be scarcely visible to the unaided eye to the large carnivorous, predatory molluscs like the tritons, helmets, and conchs. But of the many variable aspects of molluscs, none is more diverse and fascinating than the shells themselves. For here lie the unending combinations of size, shape, and color which may be assembled and preserved by collectors in an indestructible form.

Yet in spite of their differences, the members of this vast and diverse array are related to each other by a few general characteristics. They all possess a foot beneath their body and upon which they slide along. The anterior end of the body terminates in a well developed head which contains the mouth and one or two pairs of tentacles. Most snail-like molluscs possess a shell which is usually spiral in design; however, many members of this group have found their shells to be of little use to them and have been able, over a long period of time, to reduce the size of their shells and to eventually discard them.

Of nearly 200 families of gastropods, less than fifty families are included within this volume. These families are those groups which include shells of large size or embrace a large number of species and which make their home in the warm tropical waters of the Pacific and Indian Oceans.

THE LIMPET SHELL FAMILY

FAMILY PATELLIDAE

The limpets inhabit the shorelines of temperate and tropical seas. Here they are most commonly found clinging to smooth places upon the rocks in areas where they may be pounded by the surf or exposed between the tides. They are valued by the inhabitants of many localities who pry them off the rocks for the food which they offer.

The limpets are simple, conical shells with a spiral design in the young stages. The apex of the shell is slightly anterior to the middle and, unlike the key-hole limpets (Fissurellidae), is closed; from this apex ribs radiate out to cover the entire upper surface of the shell. The limpets lack the operculum which is found in many gastropod molluscs.

Upper Center

THE BLACK MOUTHED LIMPET SHELL   *Cellana melanostoma* Pilsbry

This limpet shell is tall and conical in shape, with a nearly circular base, and with steeply sloping sides which are nearly straight in outline. The sides of the shell bear well developed, rounded, radiating ribs which are occasionally crossed by fine lines. It is more usual however to find the entire outer surface of the shell somewhat eroded as shown in the figure. It is usually white or buff in color and is often marked or spotted with black. The entire interior of the shell is white or silvery except for the central callus which is nearly black in color. It will reach about two and one-half inches in diameter.

This is a fossil species occurring in the Hawaiian Islands. Some individuals regard this mollusc as a variety of *Patella sandwichensis* Pease.

Upper Row, Right and Left; Middle Row, Right and Left

THE HAWAIIAN LIMPET   *Patella sandwichensis* Pease

The individual limpets of this species vary considerably in shape and markings. In general they are conical in shape, oval at the base, and have the apex of the shell placed just anterior to the center. The surface of the shell is sculptured by between 38 and 48 radiating ribs and by intervening smaller ribs. The shell is black in color above and the ribs are usually darker than the intervening areas. The under side of the shell is of a bluish lead silvery color through which the markings of the ribs are visible. It is blackish in the center, often bordered by a lighter area and this in turn surrounded by a pattern of radiating lines. It will reach two inches in diameter. This species is known from the Hawaiian Islands.

Middle Row, Center; Lower Row

THE TALC LIMPET   *Patella talcosa* Gould

This limpet is a large species with a shell which is oval in shape at the base and which presents a conical outline when viewed from the side. The apex of the shell is placed anterior to the center and the surface, which is convex in outline, is covered by unequal radiating ribs. It is a brownish coppery color on the outside; the interior of the shell is marked by a large white central callus which is bordered by a duller area. The outer area of the lower surface is usually of a glistening silvery color through which the radiating pattern of the ribs show. It will reach about four inches in length.

This species is known from the Hawaiian Islands and doubtless elsewhere in the Pacific area.

12

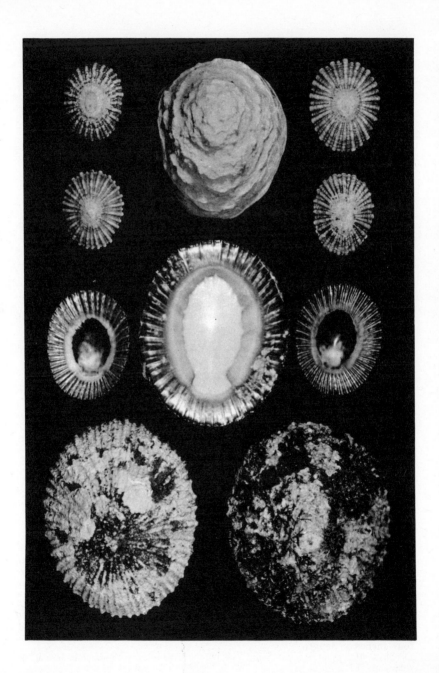

THE TOP SHELL FAMILY

FAMILY TROCHIDAE

The molluscs of this family produce heavy conical shells of iridescent, nacreous material which are covered in life by a periostracum. They are herbivorous in their habits and live among seaweed in the warm waters of the tropics.

TOP SHELL   *Trochus intextus* Kiener

This top shell is quite heavy and firm in construction and presents a fairly symmetrical, conical outline because of its large and straight spire. The entire outer surface of the shell is covered by encircling ridges, each of which bears a row of small beads upon it. The aperture is likewise spirally ridged. The shell is whitish or grayish in color and is marked over the entire outer surface with a variety of yellow, red, and brown markings. It will measure over one inch in height or diameter.

This is a common species about the Hawaiian Islands.

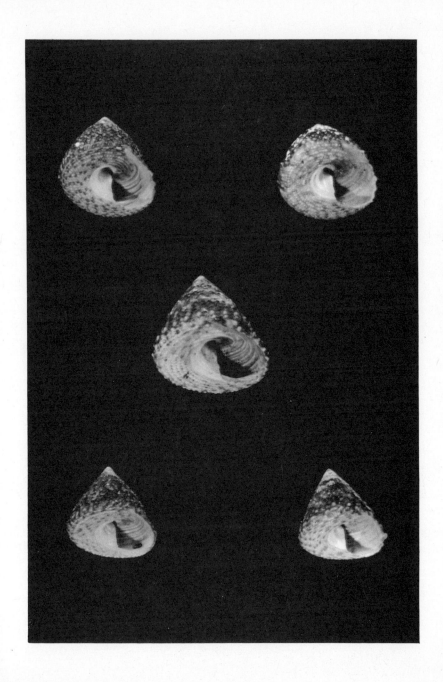

THE TURBINE SHELL FAMILY
FAMILY TURBINIDAE

These molluscs produce solid, heavy, top-shaped shells which may be either smooth, rough, or spiny on the exterior surface. The exterior is covered by a periostracum, beneath which the shell is shining and pearly. The aperture is usually oval in shape and is closed by a heavy, calcareous operculum which is flat on the inside and convex on the outside. This operculum is commonly called a "cat's eye" and is often worn as an ornament.

The members of this family are herbivorous and live along the shoreline. The group is world wide in warm water.

THE RIBBED TURBINE SHELL   *Turbo intercostalis* Menke

This turbine shell is quite heavy and solid in structure and is marked over the outside by many encircling grooves and ridges. Sometimes these ridges bear scale-like processes which in some individuals may be quite large and may project outward at an angle from the ridges. The aperture of this species is circular in outline; the operculum is also circular and usually has the external surface covered with granules. This shell is variously colored; the background color is usually greenish or gray on which are irregular markings of black, green, and brown. The outside of the operculum is usually green in the center and yellow about the border; the interior is silvery in color. This species will reach a length of about two inches.

This mollusc is distributed from the Hawaiian Islands southward and westward through the tropical Pacific Ocean.

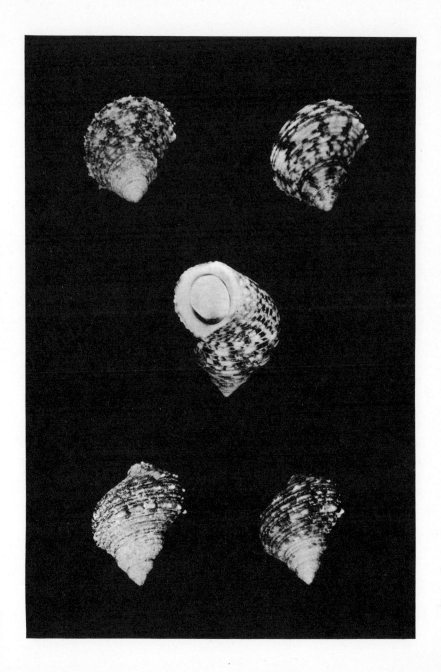

THE SEA SNAIL SHELL FAMILY
FAMILY NERITIDAE

The sea snails are a group of rather small molluscs whose shells are usually globular in shape and which have depressed spires and very large body whorls. The columella is broad and toothed, the outer lip is simple and may or may not be toothed, and the aperture is covered by a calcareous operculum.

These molluscs are vegetarians and occur along the shorelines in warm tropical waters. Some species live in the sea, some live in brackish water, a few live in fresh water, and some even live upon the land.

THE PLEATED SEA SNAIL   *Nerita plicata* Linnaeus

This sea snail is a compact, solid species of a somewhat hemispherical shape. It is covered over the outer surface with eighteen to twenty spiral ridges which are separated by grooves. The outer lip of the aperture is crenated and bears within it a row of teeth composed of a few small teeth which are bordered by a larger tooth at each end. It is whitish to brownish in color and is often spotted and streaked with black. Large specimens will reach a length of about one and one-half inches.

This mollusc is distributed from the Hawaiian Isands southward through Polynesia, and westward across the tropical Pacific Ocean to Formosa, through the East Indies, and across the Indian Ocean.

THE PITCHY SEA SNAIL   *Nerita picea* Recluz

This species is oval in shape and is marked by fine spiral lines which may be either closely or widely spaced. The columella is broad, flat, slightly concave and bears a few small teeth in the middle. The shell is dark blue to black in color and is often marked with fine, faint specks of whitish or grayish; the aperture is white. It will reach a length of about three-fourths of an inch.

This mollusc is distributed from the Hawaiian Islands southward through Polynesia and westward across the entire tropical Pacific Ocean to Japan.

Middle Row and Lower Row

THE NEGLECTED SEA SNAIL   *Nerita neglecta* Pease

This sea snail is oval in shape and is marked over the outer surface of the shell by spiral and longitudinal lines. The columella bears seven or eight teeth. The outer surface of the shell is black in color and is spotted with white; the shell is white within. It will reach a length of about one-half inch.

This species is known from the Hawaiian Islands and probably elsewhere in the Pacific area.

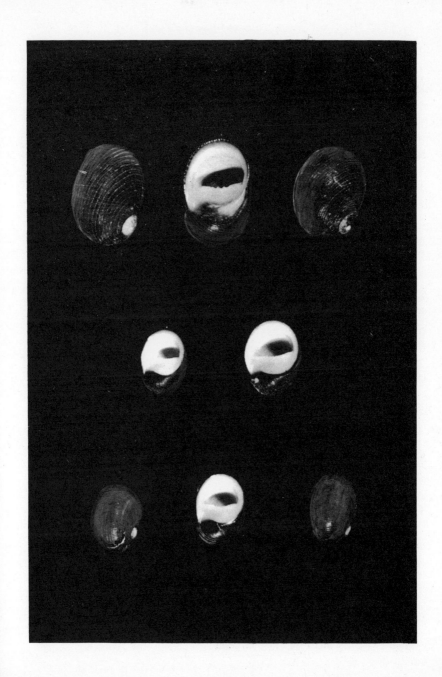

THE DECAYED NERITINA   *Clithon cariosa* (Gray)

This mollusc is compact and humped in appearance and has wing-like structures extending laterally from the lips. The columellar area is very large and the columella bears a few very fine teeth along the center and one large tooth at the posterior side. The color of the shell is dark brown or black and is flecked over the outer surface with very small yellow spots. The aperture is bluish or sometimes yellowish in color. It reaches a length of about one inch.

This species is known from the Hawaiian Islands.

THE TAHITIAN NERITINA   *Neritina tahitensis* Lesson

The shell of this species is flattened and bears large wing-like expansions on each side. The shell is thin and corneous in appearance and texture. The columellar area is large but the aperture is small. It is a light olive brown color and is without markings. It will reach a length of about one inch. This mollusc is a brackish water species and lives attached to stones in the mouths of streams.

This species is found in the Hawaiian Islands, the Samoan Islands, and in the Society Islands.

This mollusc often appears in books under the name of *N. vespertina* Nuttall.

THE GRAINED NERITINA   *Neritina granosa* Sowerby

This mollusc has a shell which is low and dome-shaped, triangular in outline, and which superficially resembles a hoof. The lips of the aperture are extended laterally to form a broad wing-like expansion which extends around three sides of the shell. The entire upper surface of the shell is covered by low, rounded tubercles. The shell is black in color above. The aperture is bluish white and speckled with darker spots. The columellar area is white, yellow, or orange in color and becomes darker toward the apex of the spire. It will reach a length of nearly two inches.

This species is known from the Hawaiian Islands where it lives attached to stones in fresh water streams.

THE PERIWINKLE SHELL FAMILY
FAMILY LITTORINIDAE

The periwinkles are fairly heavy shells of only a few whorls; these whorls may be either spiral, turbinate, or globular in shape. The aperture, which may be either oval or circular in shape, is entire along the margin and is covered by a heavy operculum. The outer lip is simple and the columella is thickened, flattened, and without an umbilicus.

The members of this group usually live among rocks in shallow water or along the shoreline. The name of the family suggests that they are littoral or shore dwelling forms.

The periwinkles are a large family and include well over 150 species which are distributed around the world.

Upper Row
THE ROUGH PERIWINKLE   *Littorina scabra* Linnaeus

The shell of this periwinkle is globular in shape, moderately thin in texture, spirally ridged, and possesses a sharp spire. The whorls are convex and slanting and the sutures between them are channelled. It is brown in color and obliquely streaked with interrupted lines; it is often yellowish or rose colored. It will exceed more than one inch in length.

This is an Indo-Pacific species ranging from the Hawaiian Islands southward to Polynesia and then westward across the entire tropical Pacific Ocean to the coast of China, through the East Indies, and across the Indian Ocean to the coast of Africa. It has been reported from the west coast of Africa and from the west coast of Mexico.

Second Row
Littorina pintado (Wood)   *Littorina pintado* Wood

This periwinkle is globular in shape and bears a short, sharp spire. The surface is spirally striate and rather smooth; the columella is broadly excavated. It is grayish or bluish white in color and is minutely dotted with purple-red dots. It ranges in length from one-fourth to three-fourths of an inch. This species occurs in Hawaii and elsewhere in the Pacific.

Third Row
Tectarius pictus (Philippi)   *Littorina picta* Philippi

This periwinkle is turbinate in shape and bears a well developed spire with a sharp apex. The whorls are convex in outline and are sometimes granulated and minutely striated. The shell is often encircled about the middle by rough, spiral ribs. It is brownish in color and marbled with white; the aperture is purple within. It will reach a length of about three-fourths of an inch. This species occurs in the Hawaiian Islands.

Some authorities regard this species as identical with *Littorina planaxis* Nuttall from California and Mexico.

A variety known as *Tectarius pictus* (Philippi) variety *marmorata* Philippi is considered to be the common form of this species.

Lower Row
THE WAVY PERIWINKLE   *Littorina undulata* Gray

This periwinkle has a firm and solid shell which may be either smooth or spirally striated. The color pattern is extremely variable and is of little help in identifying the species. It is yellowish or whitish in color and is most often marked with brown in lines, checks, spots, or in clouded patterns. The columella is always violet in color. It will reach a length of one inch.

This species is distributed from the Hawaiian Islands southward and westward through the entire tropical Pacific to the Philippine Islands, through the East Indies, and across the Indian Ocean.

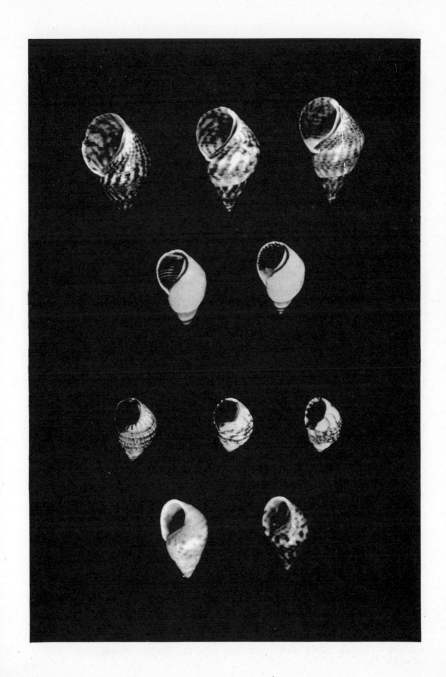

THE SUN DIAL SHELL FAMILY

FAMILY ARCHITECTONICIDAE (SOLARIIDAE)

The sun dial shells are almost circular in appearance and usually have depressed spires. They may be either conical, top shaped, or flat, depending upon the height of the spire. The aperture is angular in outline and both the columella and the lip are simple. The umbilicus of these shells is wide and deep and is marked along its margin by a knobby keel. They are found only in warm seas.

Upper Row
THE PERSPECTIVE SUN DIAL SHELL   *Architectonica perspectiva* (Linn.)

This sun dial shell is low and conical in shape. The whorls have a spiral groove below the suture and three spiral ridges at the outer edge which are separated by two grooves. The umbilicus is wide and deep and is marked by a spiral crenated ridge along the base of the whorls. The shell is white to yellowish brown in color and is encircled by rows of brown spots which appear to form disconnected lines; it is lighter in color around the edges and beneath. It will reach a diameter of two and one-half inches.

This species is distributed from the Hawaiian Islands southward to Australia and across the entire tropical Pacific Ocean to the coast of Asia, through the East Indies, and across the Indian Ocean.

Second Row
THE HYBRID SUN DIAL SHELL   *Philippia hybrida* (Linnaeus)

This sun dial shell is somewhat conical in shape, is swollen about the base and has a small umbilicus. The whorls are convex in shape, have a smooth shining surface, and bear three keels at their margins. It is encircled by a reddish brown band below the suture from which lines radiate to divide the white portion of the shell into irregular areas. It will reach a diameter of about one inch.

This species is distributed from the Hawaiian Islands southward to Australia and across the entire tropical Pacific Ocean to the Philippine Islands, through the East Indies and into the Indian Ocean.

This is a variable species. It often appears in books and collections under the name of *Solarium cingulum* Kiener.

Third Row

THE VARIEGATED SUN DIAL SHELL *Heliacus variegatus* (Gmelin)

This species exhibits a depressed shell in which the whorls are longitudinally striated and spirally grooved. The periphery of the whorl bears about ten grooves of which the one below the margin of the whorl is the largest. The umbilicus has the margin and medial rib crenulated. It exhibits a radiating pattern of white and brown; in some forms the base is white. It will exceed one-half inch in diameter.

This species extends from the Hawaiian Islands across the tropical Pacific and Indian Oceans to the Red Sea.

Several varieties of this species have been described of which *Heliacus variegatus* (Gmelin) variety *depressa* Philippi is one of the more common.

Fourth Row, Center

MIGHELS' SUN DIAL SHELL *Torinia mighelsi* Philippi

The shell of this species is much more convex than the others of this family. The whorls are four or five in number and are longitudinally striated and grooved about the periphery. The umbilicus is open and slightly crenulated along the margin. The entire shell is ashen gray in color. It will reach one-half inch in diameter.

This species is known from the Hawaiian Islands and probably elsewhere in the Pacific area.

Fourth Row, Left and Right

SUN DIAL SHELL *Torinia* species

The entire upper surface of this sun dial shell is covered by beady tubercles which are arranged in spiral rows. Each whorl bears four rows of these beads which are of equal size and a fifth or outer row which is much larger than the rest. The lower surface of the shell is marked by seven spiral beady rows, the inner two of which are by far the largest. The aperture is nearly circular in outline and is grooved within; the umbilicus is deep and open.

This is a Hawaiian species of uncertain identity. Some have suggested that it resembles *Torinia implexa* (Mighels).

Fifth Row

THE WHEEL-LIKE TOP SHELL   *Heliacus trochoideus* (Deshayes)

This sun dial shell is conically shaped and has whorls which are longitudinally striated, spirally grooved, and contain ten ribs. The ribs at the periphery are elevated, beady, and strong. The margins of the umbilicus are crenulated and its walls are marked with two spiral ribs. The shell is grayish in color and will reach three-fourths of an inch in height or diameter.

This mollusc is distributed from the Hawaiian Islands southward through Polynesia and westward across the tropical Pacific Ocean to the Philippine Islands.

THE KNOBBY SNAIL SHELL FAMILY
FAMILY APLODONIDAE (MODULIDAE)

These snails produce a somewhat flat, top-shaped shell in which the whorls are grooved and covered with tubercles. The columella in this family terminates in a tooth; a small, narrow umbilicus is also present.

This family is a small group of less than ten species all of which live in warm water.

THE COVERED KNOBBY SNAIL *Aplodon tectus* (Gmelin)

This knobby snail is top-shaped in outline and exhibits a small, depressed spire which is covered with spiral lines and rounded tubercles. The columella bears a tooth which projects into the aperture. The shell is whitish in color and is spotted with brown. It reaches a length of about one inch.

This species is distributed from the Hawaiian Islands southward throughout Polynesia, then westward across the entire tropical Pacific Ocean, through the East Indies, and across the Indian Ocean to the Red Sea.

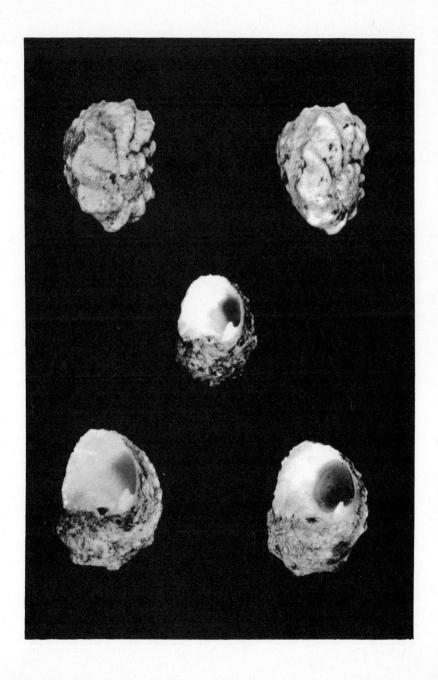

THE HORN SHELL FAMILY

FAMILY CERITHIIDAE

The horn shells are elongated in shape and are composed of many whorls, the surfaces of which are covered with tubercles. The apertures of these shells are small and oblique, bear a short anterior canal, and are covered by a horny operculum.

The horn shells are a large family consisting of more than two hundred species which live on rocks and on marine vegetation in comparatively shallow water in tropical and sub-tropical countries. They are a rather difficult group to classify.

Upper Row

THE CHINESE HORN SHELL   *Cerithium Sinense* (Gmelin)

This horn shell is encircled by spiral ribs bearing tubercles and by fine granular lines. The anterior whorl of the shell bears a prominent lateral varix and the canal at the anterior end of the aperture is curved upward. The shell is whitish in color and is decorated with brownish markings. It will reach two and one-half inches in length.

This mollusc is found from the Hawaiian Islands southward and westward throughout Polynesia, across the entire tropical Pacific Ocean, through the East Indies, and across the Indian Ocean to Mauritius.

Middle Row

THE PRICKLY HORN SHELL   *Cerithium echinatum* Lamarck

This horn shell is fairly robust in outline, of heavy construction, and presents a rough exterior. It is encircled by spiral grooves and by ridges bearing somewhat pointed tubercles. The outer lip is crenulated and is marked with purplish brown spots upon the inner surface. The shell is a light mottled brown color and bears darker brown blotches. It will reach a length of one and one-half inches.

This mollusc extends from the Hawaiian Islands southward and westward through the tropical Pacific Ocean. This shell appears to be a variable species. It appears in some collections under the name of *Cerithium mutatum* Sowerby.

Lower Row

THE COLUMNAR HORN SHELL   *Cerithium columna* Sowerby

This horn shell is moderately long in shape and presents a rough surface, encircling spiral ridges, and angular whorls which are marked by quite large low longitudinal ribs. It has a short anterior canal and a widely expanded lip. It is white to grayish in color and is marked with encircling brownish or blackish lines. It will reach one and one-half inches in length.

This species is distributed from the Hawaiian Islands southward throughout Polynesia, westward across the entire tropical Pacific Ocean to the Philippine Islands, through the East Indies, and across the Indian Ocean to Mauritius.

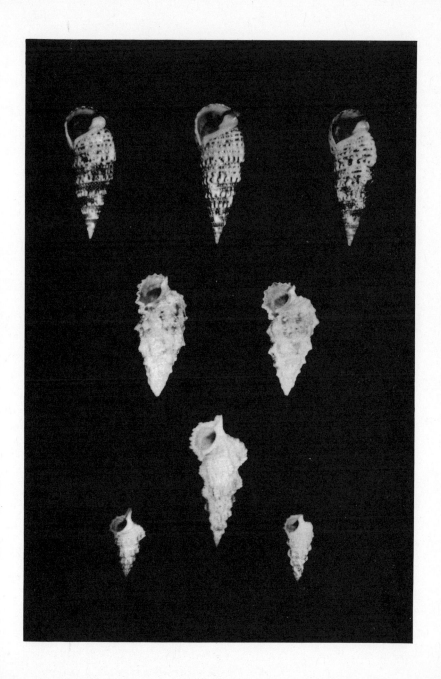

THE PHAROS HORN SHELL   *Cerithium pharos* (Hinds)

The Pharos horn shell is an elongated, slender, narrow species in which the posterior half of each whorl is longitudinally ribbed. It has a curved anterior canal, an oblique aperture, a fluted outer lip, and a columella which is thickened and bears a single plait. It is whitish in color and is variously marked with brown, usually as interrupted bands. It will reach a length of about two inches.

This species is distributed from the Hawaiian Islands southward throughout Polynesia, across the entire tropical Pacific Ocean, through the East Indies, and into the Indian Ocean.

Lower Row

HORN SHELL   *Cerithium* species

This horn shell bears a slender pointed spire and is marked by spiral grooves and by ridges which bear brown spots. The outer lip is thickened and calloused within and the inner lip likewise bears a callous. The anterior canal is curved upward at nearly ninety degrees. The color of this species varies, but it is usually of a cream color which is mottled and clouded with brown spots and blotches. It will reach a length of one and one-half inches.

This mollusc is found about the Hawaiian Islands and probably elsewhere in the Pacific area.

Upper Row

THE HAWAIIAN HORN SHELL   *Cerithium hawaiiensis* Dall

The Hawaiian horn shell is a moderately slender species which is longitudinally ribbed and grooved. The surface is also faintly spirally grooved to form a reticulated pattern of short longitudinal ridges or tubercles. It is a creamy white color and is encircled by about three narrow lines per whorl. It ranges in length from one-half to seven-eighths of an inch. This mollusc is found in the Hawaiian Islands and possibly elsewhere in the Pacific area.

Second Row, Left Pair

THE BANDED HORN SHELL   *Cerithium baeticum* Pease

This horn shell is thin in texture and is spirally encircled by shallow grooves and low ridges. It is longitudinally ribbed and covered by a pattern of beads and tubercles. The whorls are constricted at the sutures. The aperture is oval and the anterior canal is comparatively short. The shell is whitish to yellowish in color and is encircled by a wide brown line anterior to the suture and by other smaller and finer spiral lines. It will reach a length of about one-half inch.

This species is known from the Hawaiian Islands and possibly elsewhere in the Pacific area.

Second Row, Right Pair

THE BLACK MARGINED HORN SHELL   *Conocerithium atromarginatum*
                                                        (D. and B.)

This horn shell is a short stout species which is spirally grooved and ridged and which is covered over the outside by beads or tubercles. The aperture is oval, the outer lip is spotted and thickened, and the anterior canal is short. It is light in color and is mottled and clouded with various shades of brown. It will reach a length of about one-third of an inch.

This species occurs in the Hawaiian Islands and probably elsewhere in the Pacific area.

The name of *Cerithium nassoides* Sowerby is often applied to this shell.

Lower Row Right and Left

THE ISLAND HORN SHELL *Semivertagus nesioticus* (Pilsbry and Vanatta)

This horn shell is a short, solid species which is encircled by alternating larger and smaller ridges. It is white in color and is marked with faint brown spots below the sutures. It will reach a length of about three-fourths of an inch.

This mollusc is found in the Hawaiian Islands and probably elsewhere in the Pacific.

Lower Row, Center Pair

THAANUM'S HORN SHELL   *Cerithium thaanumi* Pilsbry and Vanatta

Thaanum's horn shell is a somewhat slender species in which the whorls are encircled by ridges bearing beads. The aperture is nearly circular and the lip is somewhat flaring. It will reach a length of more than one-half an inch. It is found about the Hawaiian Islands and possibly elsewhere in the Pacific area.

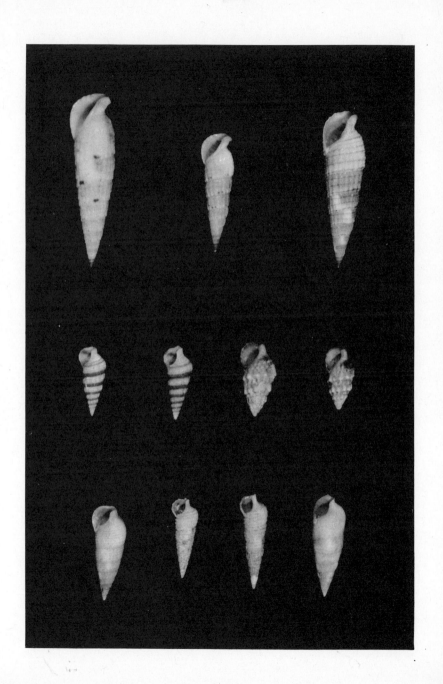

THE STAIRCASE SHELL FAMILY

Family Epitoniidae (Scalidae; Scalariidae)

The staircase shells or wentletraps are beautiful, white, polished shells with high turreted spires composed of many rounded whorls which decrease gradually in size from the body whorl to the apex of the spire. The outer surface of each whorl is covered by longitudinal varices which are formed as reflected borders of the outer lip and which become a new varix when the animal moves forward to form a new lip. In addition to a reflected border on each lip, the shell has a round aperture which is closed by a horny operculum.

Upper Row; Middle Row; Lower Row, Left and Right

The Pyramidal Staircase Shell   *Epitonium* species

This staircase shell is composed of loosely coiled whorls which are decorated over the outside by thin longitudinal ribs. The umbilicus is completely covered by the inner lip. It is whitish in color and will vary between seven-eights and one inch in length.

This species occurs in the Hawaiian Islands and probably elsewhere in the Pacific area.

The name of *Epitonium pyramis* is used by some to designate this species.

Lower Row, Center

The Pleasing Staircase Shell   *Epitonium* species

This staircase shell is composed of loosely coiled whorls which are in contact with each other. The whorls are covered over their outside by thin, longitudinal, slightly angled ribs. The umbilicus is partially covered by the lip but is open between the ribs on the ventral surface. It is white in color and will reach more than one-half inch in length.

This species is found in the Hawaiian Islands and probably elsewhere in the Pacific area.

The name of *Epitonium arestrum* is used by some to designate this species.

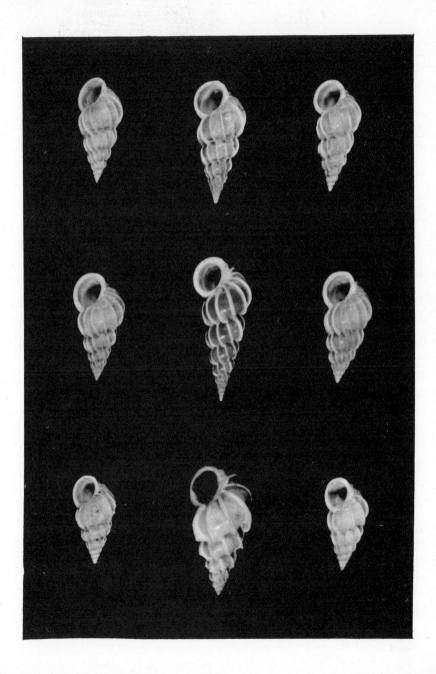

THE VIOLET SNAIL SHELL FAMILY

FAMILY JANTHINIDAE (IANTHINIDAE)

This family of molluscs is an unusual family in many ways. Its shells are among the very thinnest, the most fragile, and the most delicate of all molluscs. These creatures produce a shell of a spiral design which is lavender or purple in color and somewhat transparent. They lack an operculum.

These molluscs are also unusual in that they are pelagic or floating and drift about freely over the surface of the sea. They are gregarious in their habits and are often found singly or in groups upon a jellyfish commonly called a Portuguese-Man-O-War and on which they are reported to feed. The eggs of these snails are attached to mucous bubbles and remain floating about in the sea until they have hatched. These animals produce a bluish or purplish colored fluid which they discharge when they are disturbed.

The family is a small one and consists of less than thirty species which are distributed in both the Atlantic and Pacific Ocean.

Upper and Middle Rows

Janthina fragilis Lamarck   *Ianthina fragilis* Lamarck

The shell of this snail is globose in shape with a low spire and with the shoulder of the body whorl somewhat angular in shape. The columella is nearly straight. It is a pale violet above and a dark violet below. It has a maximum length of about one and one-half inches.

This species is world wide in warm water. It is found across the entire tropical Pacific, Indian and Atlantic Oceans and in the Mediterranean Sea.

Lower Row

Janthina globosa Swainson   *Ianthina globosa* Swainson

This violet snail is named for its globose shape. It has a low spire like the preceding species, but differs from it in having the shoulder of the body whorl rounded. It is of a whitish violet color and is darker about the spire and at the base. It will reach a length of about one and one-half inches.

This is a pelagic species which is world wide in warm water. It occurs in the Pacific, Indian, and Atlantic Oceans and in the Mediterranean Sea.

THE OBELISK SHELL FAMILY

FAMILY EULIMIDAE (MELANELLIDAE)

The obelisk shells are a large group of small, usually highly polished shells with long spires which in some species are bent toward one side. Many members of the group are parasitic in echinoderms and spend their life within the tissues of starfishes and sea urchins. Here they may be observed or often felt as a lump beneath the surface of these sea creatures. Most of the members of this family live within the tropics.

Upper Row

THAANUM'S OBELISK SHELL   *Balcis thaanumi* (Pilsbry)

Thaanum's obelisk shell is a rather solid species with an ovate aperture and with a spire which is usually slightly curved in two directions. The whorls of the shell are slightly convex and each bears an opaque varix which together unite somewhat to form a line ascending the spire on the right side and back and making in this ascent between one-fourth and one-half turns to the right. It is glistening white in color with a somewhat transparent appearance. It will reach a length of about one inch.

This species is found in the Hawaiian Islands and possibly elsewhere in the Pacific area. It is named for Mr. Ditlev Thaanum of Honolulu.

Middle Row: Right, Left, and Center

MITTRE'S OBELISK SHELL   *Stilifer mittrei* Petit

This little shell is globular in shape and has a very smooth surface. It ranges in color from a transparent white to a yellowish white color and will reach a length of about one-half inch. It is parasitic upon sea urchins, including *Echinothrix diadema* (Linnaeus).

This mollusc is distributed from the Hawaiian Islands southward throughout Polynesia, westward across the entire tropical Pacific Ocean, through the East Indies, and into the Indian Ocean.

Middle Row, Second and Fourth; Lower Row

CUMING'S OBELISK SHELL   *Balcis cumingii* (A. Adams)

This obelisk shell has a spire which is very nearly straight and contains about thirteen whorls. The varices upon the shell are irregular and are not always visible. The shell is of a white opaque color and will reach a length of about one and one-half inches.

This mollusc is distributed from the Hawaiian Islands southward through the tropical Pacific Ocean.

This is a variable species. The variety figured here is known as *Balcis cumingii* (A. Adams) variety *medipacifica* Pilsbry.

THE HOOF SHELL FAMILY

FAMILY AMALTHEIDAE (HIPPONYCIDAE)

The hoof shells are nearly all small molluscs with thick conical shells in which the apex is directed backwards. They are grayish white in color, rough in texture over the outer portion of the shell, and smooth within. The hoof shells form a base beneath them by secreting a plate upon the object to which they are attached, so that they are resting upon their own shell.

Upper Row

THE HAIRY HOOF SHELL   *Pilosabia pilosa* (Deshayes)

This hoof shell is oval or circular in outline, somewhat depressed, and has the apex of the shell placed well toward the back end of the shell. It is marked above by radial and concentric lines and has the upper surface covered by a brown pilose epidermis. The apex is usually smooth, while the lines and the epidermis become increasingly apparent toward the periphery of the shell. The margin of the aperture is smooth. The shell is white without and brownish within. Large specimens will reach three-fourths of an inch in length.

This hoof shell is distributed from the Hawaiian Islands southward throughout Polynesia and across the tropical Pacific Ocean to Japan. It is believed to occur through the East Indies and across the Indian Ocean to the coast of Africa. It is also reported from the coast of Mexico and the Galapagos Islands.

This species appears in many books under the name of *Hipponyx barbatus* Sowerby. A similar species from the Hawaiian Islands described as *Hipponyx imbricatus* Gould is believed by some to be a variety of this species.

Middle and Lower Rows

THE CONICAL HOOF SHELL   *Amalthea conica* Schumacher

The southern hoof shell is oval or nearly circular in outline and is marked over the outer surface with flat radiating ribs which are separated by narrow grooves. The circular growth lines found on some hoof shells are not apparent in this species. The prominent apex of the shell is situated near the posterior and inclines to point in a posterior direction. The outside of the shell is white in color often with brownish markings in the grooves; the interior is also tinged with brownish markings. It will reach a length of about three-fourths of an inch.

This hoof shell is distributed from the Hawaiian Islands southward to New Zealand and Australia and westward across the entire tropical Pacific Ocean to Japan, through the East Indies, and across the Indian Ocean.

THE CUP AND SAUCER LIMPET FAMILY
FAMILY CALYPTRAEIDAE

The shells of this group of molluscs are dome-shaped and, except for a slightly spiral apex, look somewhat like the limpets when viewed externally. This group is an unusual one for its members contain an internal plate or cup from which it receives its common name. The interior of these shells, including the cup, is polished and shining. There is no operculum. These molluscs live attached to solid objects, including other shells, in water ranging in depth from the shallow waters of the shoreline to deep water well beyond the reef.

THE SPINY CUP AND SAUCER SHELL   *Calyptraea spinosum* (Sowerby)

This cup and saucer shell is a difficult species to identify and to name properly because it is an extremely variable species in its form, sculpture, and coloration. It may be solid or thin, convex or depressed, circular or oval, and so on. It is usually marked over the external surface by radiating ridges which are quite thickly covered by hollow, tubular, spine-like processes of varying length. This shell varies as widely in color as it does in shape. It may be white, yellow, blue, purple, and even black in color. This species bears the characteristic cup-shaped appendage within the shell. This appendage is usually quite large in size, often laterally compressed and, although usually white in color, may be marked with a darker color in the center.

This mollusc has been recently introduced into the Hawaiian Islands by shipping. It is apparently native to the western coast of the Americas from California southward to Chile.

This species is a most confusing one and has appeared in the literature under a variety of names, the most common of which is *Crucibulum scutellatum* (Gray) variety *tubiferum* Lesson.

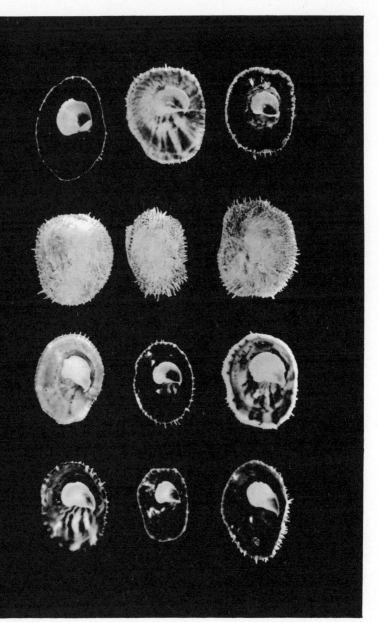

THE SPINY SLIPPER LIMPET   *Crepidula aculeata* (Gmelin)

This slipper limpet is low and dome-like in shape and oval in outline at the base. It possesses an apex which is laterally placed at the posterior end of the shell. The outer surface of the shell is marked by radiating ridges which are covered by spines of various lengths. On the lower side of the shell the columella is expanded into a shelf or septum which covers the posterior half of the aperture. This septum is usually slightly concave and its margin is usually notched in the middle and at both sides.

The color of the shell varies considerably. It ranges from white through yellowish colors to brownish above and is often marked with rays of brownish colors. The septum of the shell is white in color, while the remainder of the interior is either white or is marbled or rayed with brownish colors. This species varies in length from one to one and one-half inches.

This slipper limpet is a cosmopolitan species. It is found in the Atlantic Ocean from Florida to Argentina. In the Pacific Ocean it occurs from California to Chile, thence westward and southward to the Hawaiian Islands, Japan, Australia, and through the East Indies; it continues westward across the Indian Ocean to India and the coast of Africa.

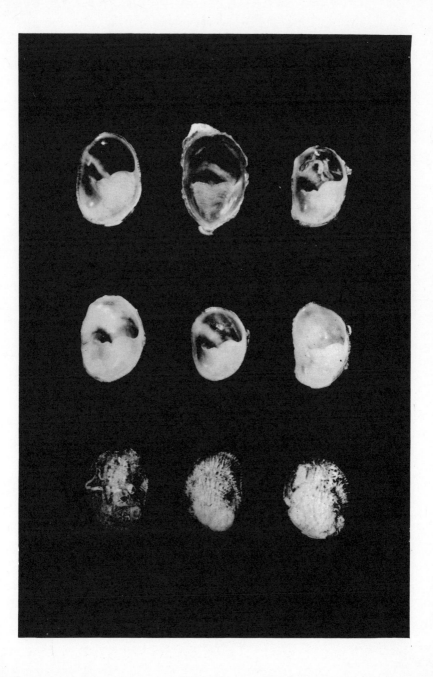

DILLWYN'S HOOF SHELL   *Cheilea dillwyni* (Gray)

This mollusc bears a shell which resembles somewhat the general pattern of the cup and saucer shells (Calyptraeidae), but it differs from them in having a basal plate beneath it. This basal plate and its attachment to a rock is shown in the top row center of the plate on the opposite page.

In general this species is circular in outline and of varying convexity. It is marked upon the upper surface by fine radiating ribs which are usually more obscure toward the apex and which become more prominent toward the margin. The margin is sometimes minutely crenulated. The central appendage or lamina, which is thickened basally and attached at the apex, is open in front and bears wing-like extensions upon the sides. The shell is usually white or yellowish in color. It will reach a diameter of about one and one-half inches.

Much confusion exists regarding this species, but it is believed to extend from the tropical western coasts of the Americas westward across the entire tropical Pacific and Indian Oceans to the coast of Africa.

This species is found in the literature under a variety of names, among them *Mitrularia equestris* Linnaeus.

HOOF SHELL OR CUP AND SAUCER SHELL   *Cheilea* species

This is a thin and fragile species of uncertain identity.

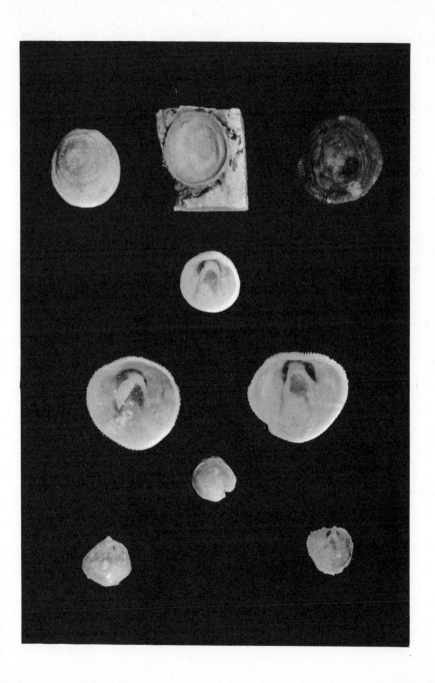

THE CONCH SHELL FAMILY

FAMILY STROMBIDAE

The conch shells are nearly all thick, solid, heavy shells with conical spires and greatly elongated body whorls. The aperture, which is long and notched at each end, is bordered on the outside by a thick outer lip which in some species is greatly expanded. The operculum of the animal is shaped like a claw and is much too small to close the aperture. This operculum together with the narrow foot is used for moving along over the bottom. They do not crawl as other snails do, but move by lifting up the shell and falling forward in such a manner that their gait is a series of leaps or jerks.

In their habits they are an active carnivorous group of snails which live upon the bottom in comparatively shallow water. The flesh of these molluscs is sometimes eaten and their shells are often made into cameos and related ornaments. Some of the members of this family are called wing shells and spider shells.

The conch shells are widely distributed about the reefs in the warm waters of the globe.

THE HAWAIIAN STROMBUS   *Strombus hawaiiensis* Pilsbry

The Hawaiian conch shell is of moderate size and has the outer lip of the shell extended laterally to form a wing-like expansion which ends posteriorly in a projection. The surface of the shell is covered by encircling ribs which are more evident at the anterior end. Each whorl also bears a single spiral row of large blunt tubercles which on the body whorl are placed just anterior to the suture. The spire is well developed and turreted. The aperture of the shell is marked with grooves which are more prominent at the anterior and posterior ends and which are weaker in the middle. The aperture of the shell is white within while the exterior surface is of a cream color speckled and marked with brownish markings which develop into bands upon the upper side of the wing-like lip. It will reach three inches in length.

As yet this species is known only from the Hawaiian Islands.

This species is regarded by some authorities as the Hawaiian form of a more widely distributed Pacific species known under a variety of names including *Strombus pacificus* Swainson, *S. aratrum* Martyn, *S. novaezelandiae* Chemnitz, *S. chemnitzii* Pfr., *S. acutus* Perry, and *S. Vomer* (Röding).

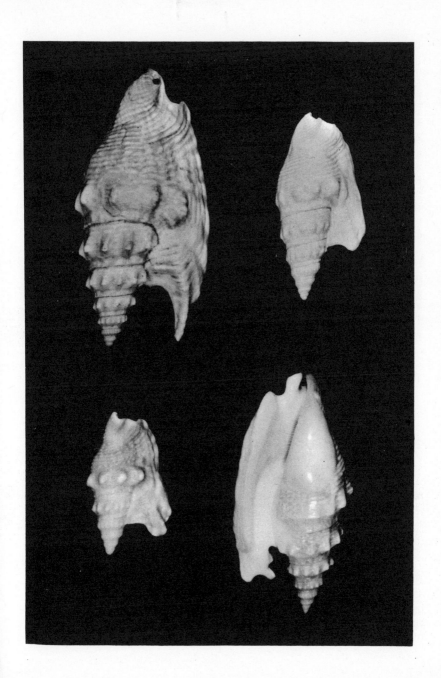

Upper Row

THE THREE TOOTHED CONCH   *Strombus tridentatus* Gmelin

This conch has an elongated shell with a smooth exterior which is marked by longitudinal ribs upon the upper part of the body whorl. The anterior margin of the outer lip bears three teeth. It is white in color and mottled with brown over the outer surface; the aperture is a vivid purple color within. It varies in length from one to one and one-fourth inches.

This mollusc extends from the Hawaiian Islands southward through Polynesia to Australia and westward across the entire tropical Pacific Ocean to the Philippine Islands.

Some individuals prefer to call this species *Strombus samar* Dillwyn.

Middle Row

HELL'S CONCH   *Strombus helli* Rousseau

This little conch has an inflated shell which is longitudinally ribbed. The aperture is narrow and ridged within and the lip is thick. It is a yellowish brown color without, while the columella and the interior are purplish. It will reach a length of about one inch.

This species extends from the Hawaiian Islands through the tropical Pacific and Indian Oceans.

Lower Row

THE SPOTTED STROMBUS   *Strombus maculatus* Nuttall

The spotted conch has a shell which is heavy in form and which exhibits a conical spire, a long aperture, and a thickened outer lip. It is spirally striated on the exterior surface; these markings become more pronounced toward the lip and the base. The outer lip is finely grooved within. The color varies but is usually white, motted or clouded with brown, yellow, or orange; it is white within the aperture. It varies in length from three-fourths to one and one-half inches.

This mollusc inhabits the area from the Hawaiian Islands southward through Polynesia and westward through the waters of the tropical Pacific Ocean, where it appears to be represented by varieties of the species.

THE MOON SHELL FAMILY

FAMILY NATICIDAE

The moon shells or shark's eyes are usually smooth and polished and have very wide apertures. The molluscs which inhabit these shells burrow along in the sand with the aid of a very large foot looking for the shell fish on which they feed. The group is world wide in warm water.

Upper Row; Lower Row, Right and Left

THE PEAR-SHAPED MOON SHELL   *Polinices pyriformis* (Recluz)

This moon shell, also known as *Polinices mamilla* (Linnaeus), is oval and conical in shape, slightly flattened, and has a smooth, polished surface. The umbilicus is covered over by a thick, heavy callosity and the operculum is thin, corneous, and pliable. The color is a beautiful pure shining white. It measures from one and one-half to two and one-half inches in length.

This species is found from the Hawaiian Islands southward throughout Polynesia, westward across the entire tropical Pacific Ocean to the Philippine Islands and through the many islands of the East Indies.

Middle Lower Row, Center 'enter

THE OPAQUE MOON SHELL   *Polinices opacus* (Recluz)

This moon shell is pointed and bears a small spire; the outer surface of the shell is smooth in texture and is marked by fine spiral lines. The operculum is thin, corneous, and pliable. This species varies widely in color; it is usually white or flesh colored, but it is often spirally banded with light brown areas. The umbilicus and the columella are always a dark chocolate or black in this species. It will reach a length of one and one-half or two inches.

This moon shell is distributed from the Hawaiian Islands southward through Polynesia, westward across the tropical Pacific Ocean to the Philippine Islands, through the East Indies, and across the Indian Ocean to the coast of Africa.

The three shells figured in the middle row are a puzzling species. They may possibly be *Polinices simiae* (Deshayes).

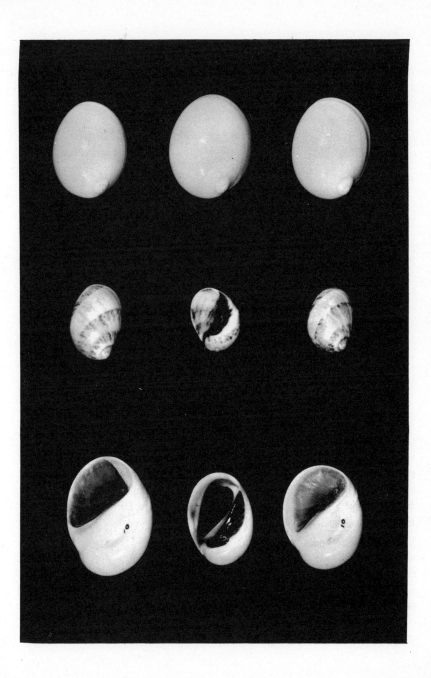

THE ARROW MOON SHELL   *Natica sagittifera* Recluz

This moon shell is regarded by some individuals as simply a color
variety of *Natica sagittata* Menke. It differs from *Natica sagittata*
Menke, however, in many other details. It is light in color and is marked
over the outer surface by wavy longitudinal lines which form two spiral
rows of darker arrow-shaped markings. The shell in the plate measures
about one-half inch in length. It is from the Hawaiian Islands.

MOON SHELL   *Natica* species

This moon shell is a species of uncertain identity. It is spirally
grooved and is marked with three rows of brownish spots upon a background of white. It measures about three-eighths of an inch in diameter.
It occurs in the Hawaiian Islands and probably elsewhere in the Pacific
area.

THE ARROW MOON SHELL   *Natica sagittata* Menke

This moon shell is somewhat oval in shape and bears a large aperture
and a wide and deep umbilicus which is nearly filled with a large callosity.
The exterior of the shell is smooth or polished and is marked with a row
of fine spirally directed wrinkles just anterior to the suture. The color
of this species is variable and may range from gray to yellow, brown, or
red. It may be of a uniform color, either light or dark, and may be
marked by encircling bands and by closely set longitudinal lines. Often
a white band follows the suture. It ranges in length from three-fourths
to one and one-half inches. The species forms a collar-like nest of mud
or sand in which to deposit its eggs; these strange formations are often
seen upon mud flats at low tide.

This species occurs from the Hawaiian Islands southward throughout Polynesia, along the northern coast of Australia, across the tropical
Pacific Ocean, through the East Indies, across the Indian Ocean to the
eastern coast of Africa, along the western coast of Africa, and in the
West Indies.

This species frequently occurs in collections under the name of *N
marochiensis* and *N. sagittifera*.

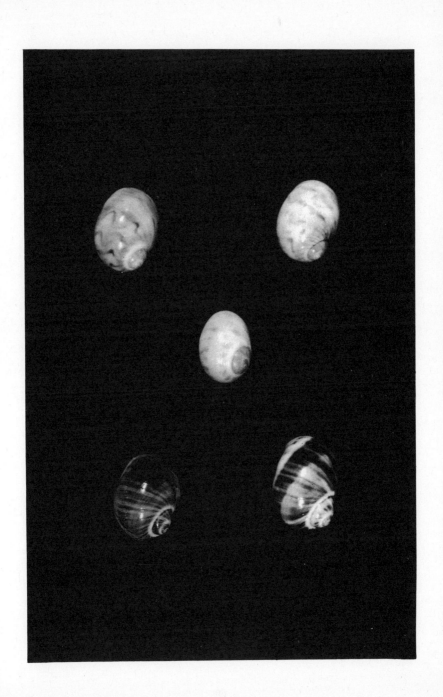

THE COWRY FAMILY

Family Cypraeidae

The cowries are the favorite group with shell collectors because of their polished enameled surfaces and beautiful color patterns. They have solid, firm shells which are of an inflated oval shape above and generally flat below. The aperture, which is narrow and margined by teeth on both sides, extends the entire length of the lower surface and terminates at each end in a narrow canal. The mantles of cowries are interesting because they consist of two lobes which extend from the bottom up over the sides of the shell to meet at the top. It is this mantle which is responsible for the beautiful exterior of the shell.

The cowries all have a spiral pattern of growth which is more apparent in young animals. As the animal matures the final whorl of the shell covers its spire so that the spire is no longer visible in the adult. When the shell reaches its maximum size, the outer lip is turned or reflected inward and thickened to form the outer half of the base of the shell. The operculum is missing.

This family is a tropical group and is not found in colder waters. It is world wide in distribution. The family includes about 200 living species.

The Tiger Cowry   *Cypraea tigris* Linnaeus

The shell of the tiger cowry is large in size, oval in shape, inflated in outline, with a flatly concave base, and with large teeth. It is a highly polished species, whitish and yellowish in color above, and marked with large black spots. The base is white. This species, one of the very largest in the family, ranges in length from two and one-half to five inches. It attains its maximum size in the Hawaiian Islands.

The tiger cowry is distributed from the Hawaiian Islands southward and westward through all of the warm tropical waters of the Pacific and Indian Oceans.

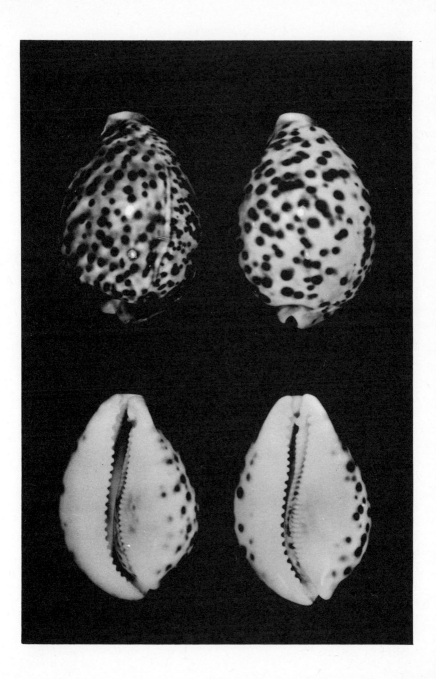

THE MAURITIUS COWRY   *Cypraea mauritiana* Linnaeus

The Mauritius cowry is a large, heavy species with somewhat angular sides, large teeth, and with a characteristic hump upon the upper surface of the shell. It is brownish in color above and marked by light brown spots; the entire lower surface is dark in color. It ranges from two and one-half to four inches in length.

This cowry is distributed from the Hawaiian Islands southward through Polynesia and westward across the tropical Pacific Ocean, through the East Indies, and across the Indian Ocean.

Center Row

THE RETICULATED COWRY   *Cypraea maculifera* Schilder

The reticulated cowry has a large, heavy, somewhat inflated shell which is strongly margined on the sides. It is brownish in color above with many regularly spaced, round, light colored spots. A large dark spot is present on the inner lip. It ranges from one and one-half to three inches in length.

This species has long been known under the name of *Cypraea reticulata* Martyn.

This cowry is distributed from the Hawaiian Islands southward and westward through all of the warm tropical waters of the Pacific and Indian Oceans.

Lower Row

THE ARABIAN COWRY   *Cypraea arabica* Linnaeus

The Arabian cowry is a large and heavy shell which is somewhat inflated and margined at the base. It is brownish in color above and is marked with light brown areas and wavy interrupted longitudinal lines; it is white in color below except at the angles of the shell and on the teeth. It will reach a length of from one and one-half to three inches.

This cowry is distributed from the Hawaiian Islands southward throughout Polynesia and westward through all of the warm waters of the Pacific and Indian Oceans.

THE YOLK OR LITTLE CALF COWRY   *Cypraea vitellus* Linnaeus

The yolk cowry has a thick shell which is oval in outline, large teeth, and a base which is somewhat rounded. The shell is olive brown and bay above and is marked with white spots; it is pure white beneath. It ranges in length from one and one-half to two and one-half inches.

This species is distributed from the Hawaiian Islands southward and westward through the tropical Pacific and Indian Oceans.

Lower Row

THE FLESH COLORED OR CARNELION COWRY   *Cypraea carneola* Linnaeus

The shell of this cowry is somewhat cylindrical in shape and fairly heavy. It is flesh colored above and is crossed by four or five bands of a deeper hue. The base and the sides of the shell are of a very dull yellowish color; the teeth are stained purple. It ranges in length from one to three inches.

This species is distributed from the Hawaiian Islands southward and westward through all of the tropical waters of the Pacific and Indian Oceans.

The mole cowry is a large species with a heavy, cylindrical, polished shell. It is a pale yellow brown color above and is crossed above by three lighter transverse bands. This shell is very dark brown or black beneath and is marked by white within the aperture and between the teeth. It ranges in length from two to nearly four inches.

This species is distributed from the Hawaiian Islands southward through Polynesia and westward across the entire tropical Pacific, through the East Indies, and across the Indian Ocean.

THE GROOVED TOOTH COWRY   *Cypraea sulcidentata* Gray

The shell of this mollusc is heavy in texture and swollen in outline, and bears a narrow aperture with very deep grooves between the teeth. It is a dull tawny color above and is often marked with bands; it is lighter in color beneath. It measures from one to two inches in length.

Although this species has been reported as distributed from the Hawaiian Islands southward through Polynesia, westward along Australia, and through the tropical waters of the Pacific Ocean, we believe that it is an endemic Hawaiian species.

SCHILDER'S COWRY   *Cypraea schiderorum* (Iredale)

The sandy cowry has a heavy shell which is oval and flattened in shape; it has a narrow aperture and is margined at the edges. It is dusky bluish in color above and is crossed by four reddish bands; the sides are ashy brown in color; the base and teeth are white. It ranges in length from one to one-half inches.

This cowry is distributed from the Hawaiian Islands southward and westward through the warm tropical waters of the Pacific Ocean.

THE CHECKERED COWRY   *Cypraea tessellata* Swainson

The checkered cowry has a shell which is thick and heavy, inflated in the center, and margined about the base. It is a yellowish brown color above and is marked on each side by two large dark brown spots. It is brownish in color beneath and the teeth are somewhat orange in color. It ranges in length from three-fourths to one and one-fourth inches.

This species has long been known as C. *arenosa* Gray.

This shell is reported to be distributed from the Hawaiian Islands southward to New Zealand and westward through the tropical Pacific Ocean. There is evidence that this species is an endemic Hawaiian form which has been developed from C. *schilderorum* and that it does not occur elsewhere in the Pacific area.

THE ERODED COWRY   *Cypraea erosa* Linnaeus

This cowry shell is oval in outline, somewhat flattened, and bears a strong margin about the base. It is grayish brown in color above and is speckled over the entire upper surface with small white spots and also by larger and less numerous brownish spots. This shell is also marked on the side at about the middle with a large conspicuous dark brownish rectangular spot. It will reach two inches in length.

This mollusc occurs from the Hawaiian Islands southward and westward across the entire tropical Pacific and Indian Oceans.

THE ISABELLA COWRY   *Cypraea isabella* Linnaeus

The Isabella cowry is very light in weight and cylindrical in form with a narrow aperture and many teeth. It is a bluish yellow color above and is faintly banded and marked by small black longitudinal spots. It is marked with deep red at the extremities; the under surface is white. It ranges in length from three-fourths to one and one-half inches.

This cowry is distributed from the Hawaiian Islands southward and westward across the entire tropical Pacific and Indian Oceans.

THE LYNX COWRY   *Cypraea lynx* Linnaeus

The lynx cowry has a heavy pear-shaped shell with a narrow flat base. It is whitish in color above, but is very thickly spotted and clouded with brownish, yellowish, and bluish colors. The sides and the base of the shell are white; it is tinged with red between the teeth. It varies in length from three-fourths to two and one-half inches.

Some authors prefer to use the name of *Cypraea vanelli* Linnaeus for this species.

The lynx cowry is distributed from the Hawaiian Islands southward through Polynesia and westward along the coast of Australia, through all of the tropical waters of the Pacific Ocean, through the East Indies, and across the Indian Ocean to the Red Sea.

Upper Right and Left

THE JESTER COWRY   *Cypraea scurra* Gmelin

The jester cowry is of medium size, somewhat cylindrical in form,
slightly elongated at the ends, and bears fine numerous teeth. It is a
bluish gray color and is covered by a reticulated pattern of brown lines;
the sides are brownish and are speckled with black spots. It ranges from
one and one-fourth to two inches in length.

This species is distributed from the Hawaiian Islands southward to
Australia and westward through the tropical Pacific Ocean.

Upper Center

THE CYLINDRICAL COWRY   *Cypraea cylindrica* Born

The cylindrical cowry was named for its elongated shape. It is a
species of medium size with the sides and extremities margined, with large
outer teeth, and with smaller inner teeth which may extend part way over
the base of the shell. It is bluish in color above and is marked over the
upper surface by many fine brownish spots and by a large dark irregularly
shaped blotch. Two dark brownish spots mark each end of the upper surface; the lower surface is white in color. It will reach a length of one
and one-half inches.

This mollusc is distributed throughout the tropical Pacific Ocean,
through the East Indies, and into the Indian Ocean. It has been brought
into the Hawaiian Islands on the hulls of ships.

Middle Row, Right and Left

THE SMOOTH OR TAPERING COWRY   *Cypraea teres* Gmelin

This cowry shell is elongate, small in size, depressed at the base,
margined on the right side, and has a narrow aperture and small teeth.
It is whitish in color and is crossed above by three poorly defined bands of
short, wavy, longitudinal, pale brown lines. It ranges in length from three-
fourths to one inch.

This mollusc is distributed from the Hawaiian Islands southward and
westward across the entire tropical Pacific Ocean, through the East Indies,
and into the Indian Ocean.

This species is also known under the name of *C. tabescens* Dillwyn.

Lower Center; Lower Row, Right and Left

THE SIEVE COWRY   *Cypraea cribraria* Linnaeus

This cowry is a medium sized species of light weight and beautiful design. It is a yellowish brown color above and is marked over the entire
upper surface with round white spots. The entire base, the extremities,
and the sides are white in color. It will reach a length of about one and
one-fourth inches.

This species is distributed throughout the tropical Pacific Ocean,
through the East Indies, and into the Indian Ocean. It has been brought
into the Hawaiian Islands on the hulls of ships.

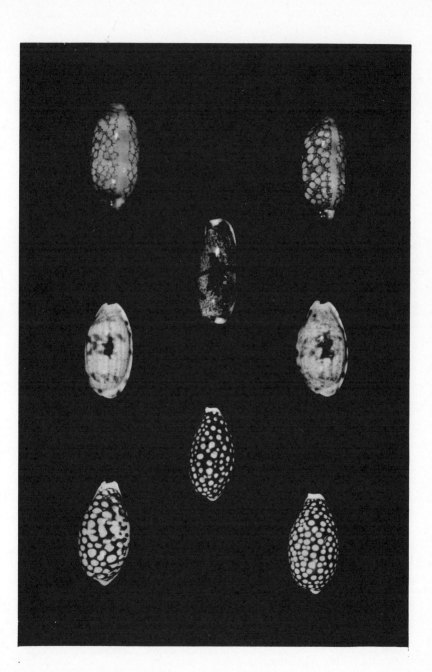

THE POROUS COWRY   *Cypraea poraria* Linnaeus

This cowry is quite thick, small in size, oval in shape, and is slightly margined about the base. It is a brownish purple color and is covered over the upper surface by small white spots most of which are set within a larger brownish spot. The sides and much of the base are of a violet color; the teeth are white. It will reach one inch in length.

This mollusc is known to occur from the Hawaiian Islands southward and westward through all of the tropical Pacific and Indian Oceans.

THE GRAPE OR GRAPE SHOT COWRY   *Cypraea staphylaea* Linnaeus

This cowry is a small oval species which resembles *C. poraria* in some respects. Specimens which have not developed pustules upon them so closely resemble *C. poraria* that they cannot be easily distinguished from above. Unlike *C. poraria*, however, the teeth of this species extend over the base forming grooves and ridges. This is apparently a variable species ranging from gray to brown and bears white pustules tipped with reddish-brown in varying stages of development and prominence. It will reach a length of about one inch.

This cowry is distributed across the tropical Pacific and Indian Oceans. It has been brought into the Hawaiian Islands on the hulls of ships.

THE RED OR HONEY COLORED COWRY   *Cypraea helvola* Linnaeus

The red cowry is a small, oval, flattened, margined species with large teeth which extend onto the outer lip. It is brownish in color above and is marked over the upper surface by many small white spots and larger brown spots. It is of a reddish brown color over the entire under surface. It ranges in length from one-half to one and one-fourth inches.

The red cowry is distributed from the Hawaiian Islands southward and westward across the entire tropical Pacific and Indian Oceans.

THE HALF-SWIMMER COWRY   *Cypraea semiplota* Mighels

The shell of this cowry is small in size, oval in shape, margined, and has a narrow aperture. It is olive brown in color above and is marked over the upper surface by many small white spots. It is light in color below with a yellowish aperture. It will reach a length of about three-fourths of an inch.

This cowry is believed to be restricted in its distribution to the Hawaiian Islands.

A broader heavier shell often known as *C. annae* Roberts is a variety of this species. *C. polita* Roberts also seems to be identical with this species.

Upper Row; Middle Row, Left and Right; Lower Row

THE FRINGED COWRY   *Cypraea fimbriata* Gmelin

The fringed cowry has a small, oval, shell with a flat base which is somewhat margined; the teeth are quite small and the aperture becomes wider anteriorly. It is light bluish in color above with a large central darker area. It is finely speckled above with brown and is marked above with two brown spots at each extremity; it is whitish below. It ranges in length from one-half to one inch.

This species is distributed from the Hawaiian Islands southward through Polynesia, westward through the tropical Pacific Ocean, through the East Indies, and into the Indian Ocean.

Middle Row, Center

THE OSTERGAARD COWRY   *Cypraea ostergaardi* Dall

This cowry is a small species which is quite oval in outline and pitted along the margin. The teeth are small and extend only a short way onto the base. It is whitish in color and is evenly marked above with brown spots; the base is white. It varies in length from one-half to three-fourths of an inch. This shell is named for Mr. Jens Mathias Ostergaard, for many years in the Department of Zoology at the University of Hawaii.

This species is known only from the Hawaiian Islands.

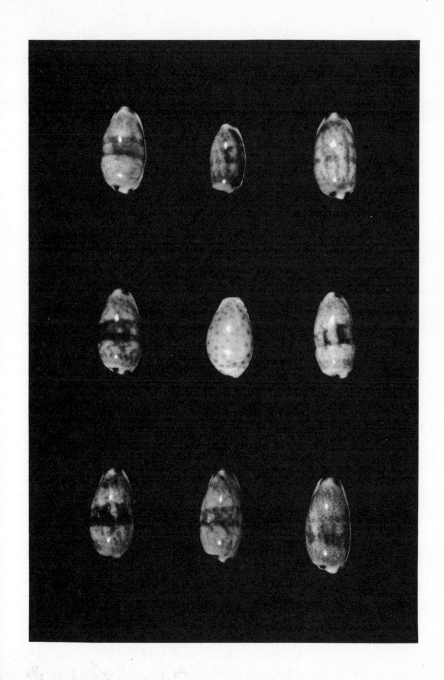

ANNA'S COWRY   *Cypraea annae* Roberts

Some individuals regard this cowry as a broad, heavy, flattened variety of *Cypraea semiplota* Mighels. Although it resembles this species in many ways it differs from *C. semiplota* in its shape and to a lesser degree in its color patterns. It measures about one-half inch in length.

This cowry is found in the Hawaiian Islands.

Second Row

THE MONEY COWRY   *Cypraea moneta* Linnaeus

The money cowry has a shell of medium size which is somewhat flattened and triangular in shape; its margins are thick and often bear tubercles at the base. It is usually yellowish in color above and below and often contains white over large areas of the shell; it is sometimes marked above by a faint red ring. It ranges in length from one-half to one and one-half inches.

This cowry is distributed from the Hawaiian Islands southward and westward across the entire tropical Pacific and Indian Oceans.

Third Row

RASHLEIGH'S COWRY   *Cypraea rashleighana* Melvill

This cowry is a small, somewhat oval, slightly flattened species which bears a small margin about the base. It is quite oval in outline beneath and exhibits a fairly wide aperture and medium sized teeth. It is a light grayish brown color above and is marked above with one, two, three, or four interrupted brownish bands. It is also marked above the margins by small brownish spots. It is entirely white beneath. It approaches three-fourths of an inch in length.

This species occurs in the Hawaiian Islands and in central Polynesia.

This cowry was named by Mr. Melvill in honor of his friend Mr. Jonathan Rashleigh, a student of cowries, who died in 1872 at the age of twenty-seven years.

Lower Row

THE SNAKE HEAD COWRY   *Cypraea caputserpentis* Linnaeus

The snake head cowry is oval in outline, of a sturdy, flattened design, and has well developed teeth. It is a deep reddish brown color around the sides, white on the extremities and on the teeth, and is covered over the upper surface by a large number of white spots of various sizes. The young of this species is difficult to recognize because its upper surface is usually crossed by a single wide band upon an ashy background. Large adult specimens will approach an inch in length.

This cowry is the most common member of its family in the Hawaiian Islands. It is distributed from the Hawaiian Islands southward and westward across the entire tropical Pacific and Indian Oceans.

The Chinese Cowry   *Cypraea chinensis* Gmelin

The upper surface of this cowry is bluish white in color and is marked with light orange brown reticulations; the sides are creamy white and marked by round purple spots. The teeth of the outer lip extend onto the lower surface of the shell while the teeth of the inner lip are limited to the aperture. The teeth are white with bright orange interstices. It will reach a length of about one and one-half inches.

This cowry ranges from the Hawaiian Islands southward and westward throughout the tropical Pacific Ocean and extends into the Indian Ocean.

This species is found in some collections under the name of *Cypraea cruenta* Dillwyn.

Upper Center and Lower Center

The Actor Cowry   *Cypraea histrio* Gmelin

This cowry is a difficult and confusing one to identify because it so closely resembles *C. maculifera*, *C. arabica* Linnaeus, and *C. intermedia* Gray. Of these three species, it most closely resembles *C. maculifera* but it differs from this species in being more elongated, in having smaller margins, and in having a white base. It will reach a length of nearly three inches.

This cowry is distributed from the Hawaiian Islands southward throughout Polynesia, along the coast of Australia, westward across the entire tropical Pacific Ocean, and into the Indian Ocean.

Center Row

The Eroded Cowry   *Cypraea erosa* Linnaeus

This species is described elsewhere within this family. See page 70.

Lower Row

The Smooth or Tapering Cowry   *Cypraea teres* Gmelin

This species is described elsewhere within this family. See page 72.

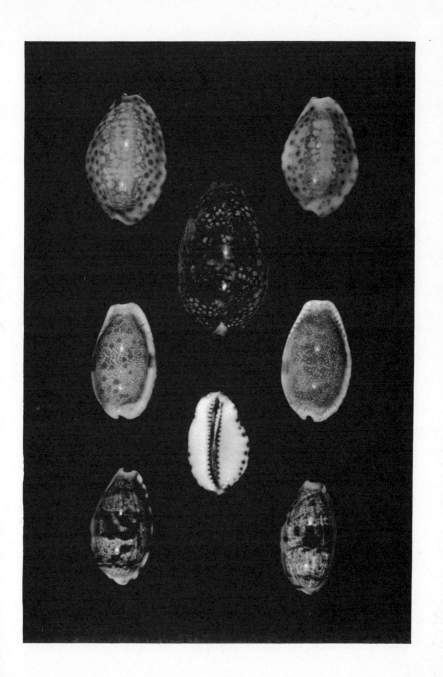

THE CHICK PEA COWRY   *Cypraea cicercula* Linnaeus

This little cowry is most easily recognized by the fact that its extremities are drawn out at both ends to form slender processes. It is globular in shape with a humped appearance and is grooved in the middle of the shell above. The aperture is narrow and bears fine teeth which extend onto the base. It is glassy yellowish white in color above and is blotched with brown; the sides are dotted with brown. It ranges in length from one-half to three-fourths of an inch.

This species is distributed from the Hawaiian Islands southward throughout Polynesia and westward across the tropical Pacific and Indian Oceans.

Second Row

THE RING COWRY   *Cypraea annulata* Gray

The ring cowry is oval in outline and plump in form with a smooth surface and with very fine teeth along the aperture. It is a whitish ivory color and is marked over the upper surface by yellowish spots which are encircled by slightly darker colored rings. The lower side or base of the shell is entirely white. It measures about one-half inch in length.

This cowry is distributed from the Hawaiian Islands southward and westward across the entire tropical Pacific and Indian Oceans to Mauritius.

Third Row

GASKOIN'S COWRY   *Cypraea gaskoini* Reeve

Gaskoin's cowry is an oval, fairly solid species which is margined about the base and which has quite strong teeth. It is a straw yellow color above and is marked over the entire upper surface with brown-ringed white spots; the sides are dotted with brown. It ranges from one-half to three-fourths of an inch in length.

This cowry inhabits the waters about the Hawaiian Islands and extends southward into Polynesia.

Fourth Row

THE NUCLEAR COWRY   *Cypraea nucleus* Linnaeus

This little cowry is oval in outline and has the extremities of the shell extended as a pair of blunt processes. The upper surface is covered by nodules, many of which are connected by narrow ridges. The base of the shell is covered by transverse lines or ridges. It is whitish in color and is marked with brown. It ranges from one-half to three-fourths of an inch in length.

This species is distributed from the Hawaiian Islands southward throughout Polynesia and westward across the entire tropical Pacific and Indian Oceans.

Lower Row

THE MADAGASCAR COWRY   *Cypraea granulata* Pease

The Madagascar cowry is flattened, oval in outline, and usually bears a margin about the base of the shell. The upper surface is covered by nodules, while the lower surface is marked by transverse ridges which on the outer lip may be alternately larger and smaller. It is brownish and whitish in color. It will reach a length of a little more than one inch.

This cowry is found in the Hawaiian Islands.

THE HELMET SHELL FAMILY

FAMILY CASSIDIDAE

Helmet shells are nearly all large, thick, heavy shells which are triangular in shape on the under side. The spire is short and the aperture is usually long and leads into an anterior canal which in some species is curved upward and backward. The operculum is small and horny. The outer lip is thickened and usually toothed on its inner margin. The animals live on sandy bottoms in tropical waters where they crawl along in search of other molluscs on which they feed. Some species of this family are sought after commercially to be later made into cameos.

The family of the helmet shells includes more than twenty-five species.

THE HORNED HELMET SHELL   *Cassis cornuta* (Linnaeus)

This helmet shell is very large and heavy and is marked over the outer surface with three rows of spiral tubercles, of which the posterior row is by far the largest. The surface of the shell has a honey-combed pattern which may be obscured by marine growth.

The shell is creamy white above, orange brown in the aperture, and has white teeth. It will reach a length of eight to twelve inches. It is the largest mollusc found in the Hawaiian Islands.

This species is distributed from the Hawaiian Islands southward and westward throughout Polynesia, through the entire tropical Pacific Ocean to Japan and the Philippine Islands, through the East Indies, and across the Indian Ocean to the coast of Africa. It also inhabits the West Indies.

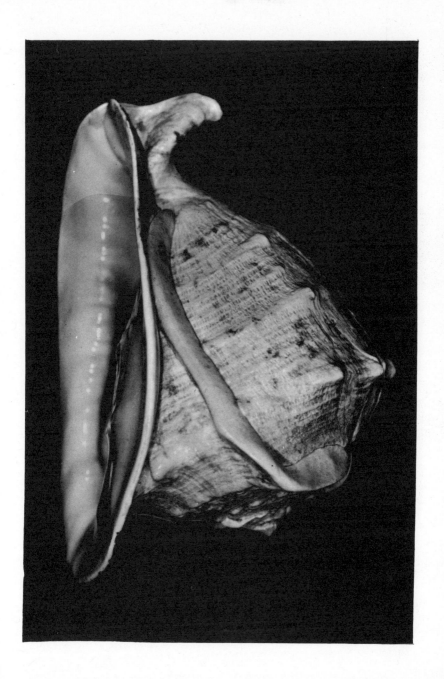

THE SPINY HELMET SHELL   *Casmaria erinaceus* (Linnaeus)

This helmet shell is globular in shape and presents a smooth surface both inside and outside. The anterior lip is thickened and is bordered anteriorly by a few small teeth or spines. It is white or brownish white in color and is marked by three faint spiral brown bands and by brown spots on the suture and along the lip. From one to three inches long.

This species is distributed from the Hawaiian Islands southward and westward through Polynesia, through all of the warm tropical waters of the Pacific Ocean to the East Indies, and across the Indian Ocean to the coast of Africa.

THE STRIPED HELMET SHELL   *Casmaria erinaceus* (Linn.)
                                          v. *Kalosmodix* (Melvill)

This helmet shell like the preceding species is globular in shape, smooth within and without, and has a thickened outer lip. It is white or brownish-white in color and is marked with faint longitudinal stripes and brown bands. The lips are marked with dark brown spots. It varies from one to three inches in length.

This species is distributed from the Hawaiian Islands southward and westward through all of Polynesia, across the entire tropical Pacific Ocean, through the islands of the East Indies, and across the Indian Ocean to the coast of Africa. Some individuals regard this species as a variety of *Casmaria erinaceus* (Linnaeus).

THE PONDEROUS HELMET SHELL   *Casmaria ponderosa* (Gmelin)

This little helmet shell is smooth over the outer surface. The whorls are angled at the shoulder and possess a spiral row of low tubercles which extend anteriorly as folds onto the body whorl. The outer lip is wide and thick and bears a row of small, sharp tubercles along its outer and lower margin. The shell is white in color and is marked about the sutures by brown spots. The upper side of the outer lip is marked by a series of rectangular brown spots. It will reach a length of about one and one-half inches. This species is distributed from Hawaii southward through Polynesia and westward across the entire tropical Pacific Ocean to Ryukyu and the Philippine Islands.

THE STRONGLY GROOVED HELMET SHELL   *Semicassis fortisulcata*
                                          (E. A. Smith)

This helmet shell is spherical in shape, thin, small in size, and has the external surface evenly marked by deep spiral grooves. It is white in color and faintly blotched with brown. It ranges in length from one to two inches. It is known from the Hawaiian Islands and possibly elsewhere in the Pacific Ocean area.

THE TRITON SHELL FAMILY

FAMILY CYMATIIDAE (TRITONIDAE; SEPTIDAE)

The tritons are a large family of thick, rugged, strong shells which exhibit a spiral pattern of growth. These shells bear a decorative pattern over their exteriors and have never more than one or two varices to a whorl. The shells of this family all exhibit a prominent anterior canal and usually have teeth upon the inner surface of the outer lip. The operculum is present.

The members of this family inhabit the bottom from the shoreline to depths of three hundred feet or more and are found in both tropical and temperate waters.

TRITON'S TRUMPET   *Tritonalia tritonis* (Linnaeus)

Triton's trumpet is one of the largest and most beautiful shells in the sea. It is easily recognized by its large size and by the fact that its shell is marked by encircling ribs, low rounded varices, a long spire, and a large body whorl with a still larger aperture. It is colored on the outside of the shell by white, yellow, and brown; this color is often disposed in rows of moon shaped blotches. The aperture is usually reddish orange within, while the columella is of a dark chocolate color crossed by light plications. It will reach a length of at least sixteen inches.

This species is distributed from the Hawaiian Islands southward throughout Polynesia and the south seas to New Zealand, westward to Japan and the Philippine Islands, through the islands of the East Indies, and into the Indian Ocean.

THE QUILTED OR KNOBBY TRITON   *Cymatium tuberosum* (Lamarck)

The shell of this triton is spirally ribbed and covered by six or more rounded varices. The anterior canal is quite long and is curved upwards. The outer lip and the columella are heavily coated with enamel. It is brownish in color without and orange or reddish within the aperture. It will reach two and one-half inches in length.

This species is found from the Hawaiian Islands southward through Polynesia, westward through the islands of the tropical Pacific Ocean, through the East Indies, and across the Indian Ocean to the coast of Africa. It is also reported from the West Indies.

Upper Center

THE PEAR TRITON   *Cymatium pyrum* (Linnaeus)

The pear triton is transversely ribbed and is marked by four varices. The anterior canal is rather long and curved, while the spire is shorter than most other members of this group. The aperture bears teeth upon the outer lip. In color this species is yellowish orange or red, often with white spots upon the varices. The aperture and teeth are light colored or white.

This species is found from the Hawaiian Islands southward through Polynesia, westward through the islands of the tropical Pacific Ocean, through the Philippine Islands and the East Indies, and across the Indian Ocean to Madagascar and the coast of Africa.

Middle Row, Left and Right

THE BEADED OR GEM TRITON   *Cymatium gemmatum* (Reeve)

The beaded triton is marked by longitudinal varices and by revolving ribs and striae which are sometimes crossed by longitudinal ribs; it often bears two or three nodules between the varices. The shell varies from whitish to orange yellow in color. It will reach a length of one and one-half inches.

This species is distributed from the Hawaiian Islands southward and westward throughout Polynesia and the islands of the tropical Pacific Ocean to the Philippine Islands.

Lower Row

THE LITTLE RED TRITON   *Cymatium rubecula* (Linnaeus)

The surface of this shell is marked with six prominent varices and by spiral granulose ridges about the whorls. This species varies in color between a lemon and an orange red. It is often marked with a whitish or yellowish band about the middle of the body whorl, and the varices are banded with spots of white. The lips and the columella resemble the exterior of the shell in color, but the teeth and the interior of the shell are usually white. It will reach a length of two inches.

This mollusc is distributed from the Hawaiian Islands southward and westward through all of the islands of the tropical Pacific Ocean to the Philippine Islands, through the East Indies, and across the Indian Ocean to the Red Sea and the coast of Africa. It is also reported from the West Indies.

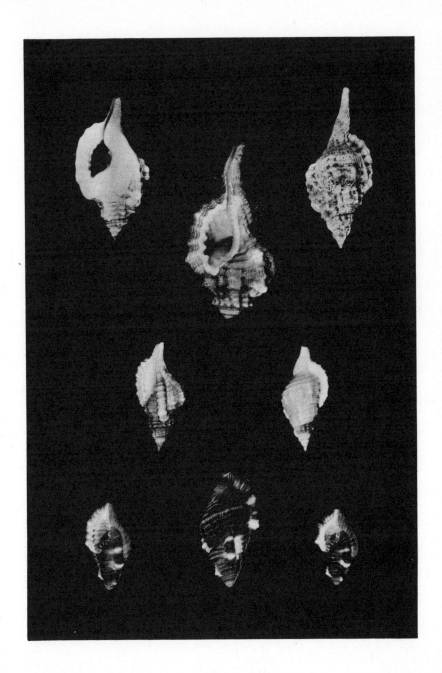

Upper Row

THE HAIRY TRITON   *Cymatium pileare* (Linnaeus)

The hairy triton is marked with spiral ribs and with seven to nine varices which are separated by three to five longitudinal rows of tubercles. It is covered by a thin, brown, bristly epidermis.

This shell is whitish, yellowish, and brownish in color, often in the form of revolving bands; the aperture is orange red with white plications. It measures between two and five inches.

This species is distributed from the Hawaiian Islands southward and westward through Polynesia and the many islands of the tropical Pacific Ocean, along the coast of Australia, Japan, and China, through the East Indies, and across the Indian Ocean to the Red Sea.

Middle Row, Left and Right

THE INTERMEDIATE TRITON   *Cymatium intermedia* (Pease)

The identity of this species is very much in doubt. It is a form found in the Hawaiian Islands.

Middle Row, Center

THE CLANDESTINE OR HIDDEN TRITON *Cymatium clandestinum* (Lamarck)

This triton has well rounded whorls which usually bear a single longitudinal varix and which are encircled by many regular revolving cord-like ribs. The outer lip bears teeth upon its inner margin. The shell is a light yellowish brown color without and white in color within. The revolving ribs and the teeth are darker brown in color. This species reaches about two and one-half inches in length.

This triton is distributed from the Hawaiian Islands southward and westward through the islands of the tropical Pacific Ocean to Australia, Guam, and the Philippine Islands.

Lower Row

THE NICOBAR TRITON   *Cymatium nicobaricum* (Röding)

This triton is a large and fairly heavy species which is marked with the usual revolving ribs and longitudinal varices. The shell is whitish in color and is marked with reddish or brownish spots; the lips, aperture, and the columella are bright orange in color. It ranges in length from one and one-half to three inches.

This species is distributed from the Hawaiian Islands southward and westward through Polynesia and the islands of the south seas to the Philippine Islands, through the East Indies, and across the Indian Ocean to the Red Sea and the coast of Africa.

The shell of this species is covered with spiral rows of tubercles which are arranged to form a network over the surface of the shell. The columellar side of the aperture is covered by a large calloused area. The aperture is bordered with many teeth. The color is nearly white externally, but is often marked with reddish brown bands. It ranges in length from two to three inches.

This species extends from the Hawaiian Islands southward throughout Polynesia, along northern Australia, and then westward through the islands of the south seas, through the Philippine Islands and the East Indies, and across the Indian Ocean to the Red Sea and the coast of Africa.

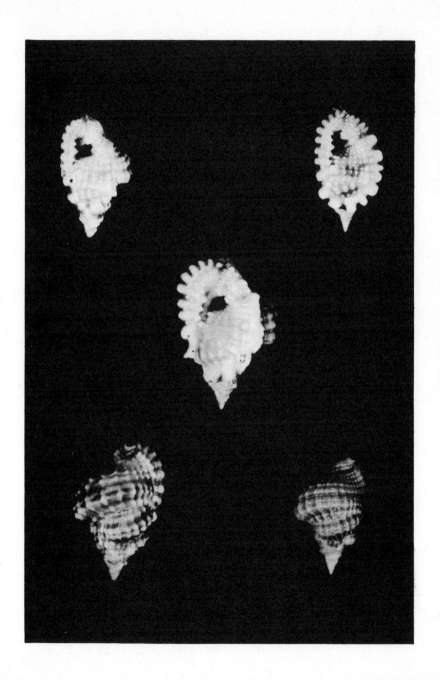

THE DISTORTED SERPENT SHELL   *Colubraria distorta* (Sch. and Wag.)

This serpent shell is elongated, thick, and solid; the spire is bent; and the whorls are covered by granules and contain about nine obliquely placed varices. The color of this species is usually pinkish or yellowish-brown and is marked with chestnut brown areas and spots. It ranges in length from one and one-half to two and one-half inches.

This species is distributed from the Hawaiian Islands southward throughout Polynesia, westward through the islands of the tropical Pacific Ocean, through the East Indies, and into the Indian Ocean.

This species is often found in the literature under the name of *Triton distorta* Sch. and Wag.

THE TWISTED SERPENT SHELL   *Colubraria strepta* (Cossman)

This serpent shell is a smaller species than the other forms described here. It is slender in outline with a slightly curved spire and with a comparatively small aperture. It is about one inch in length.

This species is found about the Hawaiian Islands and possibly elsewhere in the Pacific area.

THE POINTED SERPENT SHELL   *Colubraria muricata* (Humphrey)

This shell is elongated in form and has a somewhat turreted spire which is marked with about eleven varices. It appears to be longitudinally grooved and encircled by rows of tubercles. The anterior canal is short, the columella is smooth and thickly enamelled, and the outer lip is toothed within. It is of a light brownish color and is marked with chestnut brown areas and with one or two encircling rows of brown spots. It ranges in length from one and one-half to two and one-half inches.

This species seems to be world wide in warm water. It extends from the Hawaiian Islands southward throughout Polynesia, westward through the tropical Pacific Ocean, through the East Indies, and into the Indian Ocean. It is also reported from the Cape Verde Islands off the west coast of Africa and from the West Indies.

This mollusc often appears in books under the name of *Triton obscurus* Reeve.

THE RIDGED TRITON OR FROG SHELL FAMILY

FAMILY BURSIDAE

This family of shells resembles the family of the triton shells in many ways and is often included in that group. They differ from the tritons in having large longitudinal ridges on opposite sides of the shell. These ridges are really the thickened lip of the shell which has been left behind as the animal grew larger, moved farther along, and formed new lips as it continued to grow.

Upper Row and Lower Row

THE TOAD LIKE TRITON *Bursa bufonia* (Gmelin)

This species is marked by a curved canal at each end of the aperture. It is white in color, spotted with brown on the outside and white or yellowish within. It will reach a length of two and one-half inches.

This triton is found from the Hawaiian Islands southward through Polynesia, westward through the islands of the tropical Pacific Ocean, through the East Indies, and across the Indian Ocean to the Red Sea and the coast of Africa.

Bursa siphonata (Reeve) and *Bursa mammata* Röding are regarded by some individuals as varieties of this species and by others as separate yet closely related species. Both have the outer and columellar lip colored with purple rather than white.

Center

THE LAMP TRITON *Bursa lampas* (Linnaeus)

The lamp triton is a large species with a well developed, turreted spire; it has more than ten varices upon the shell and in addition bears two prominent and several less prominent rows of tubercles upon each whorl together with smaller revolving granular ridges. The columella is wrinkled and the outer lip is toothed. The shell is whitish to cream colored and is clouded with orange brown; it is flesh colored within. It ranges in length from three to nine inches.

This mollusc is found from the Hawaiian Islands southward and westward through the tropical Pacific Ocean, through the islands of the East Indies, and across the Indian Ocean to the Red Sea and the coast of Africa.

THE RELATED TRITON   *Bursa affinis* Broderip

This triton is marked by varices on opposite sides of the shell and by
spiral rows of tubercles which cover the shell; of the several rows of
tubercles, the center row on each whorl is the largest. The color of this
shell ranges from fleshy white to yellowish; the apex is rosy and the
surface is spotted and stained with brownish red. It will reach two
inches in length.

This species is found from the Hawaiian Islands southward and west-
ward through Polynesia, the islands of the south seas and through the
Philippine Islands and the East Indies. It is also reported from the
West Indies.

Middle Row

THE BLOOD SPOTTED TRITON   *Bursa cruentata* (Sowerby)

This species is of a whitish, yellowish, or brownish color and is
covered by tubercles, the larger of which are often spotted with red;
the aperture is white or rosy in color within; and red spots sometimes
mark the columella. It will reach a length of one and one-half inches.

The range of this mollusc extends from the Hawaiian Islands southward and westward through the many islands of the tropical Pacific
Ocean to the Philippine Islands, through the East Indies, and across the
Indian Ocean to Mauritius and the coast of Africa. It is also reported
from the West Indies.

Lower Row

THE SPOUTED TRITON   *Bursa siphonata* (Reeve)

This triton resembles in many ways the species known as *Bursa bufonia* (Gmelin) and is by many authorities regarded as a synonym, or
at most a variety, of that species. This species differs from *B. bufonia*
in having the columellar lip colored purple rather than white; in other
characters it appears to be identical with *B. bufonia*.

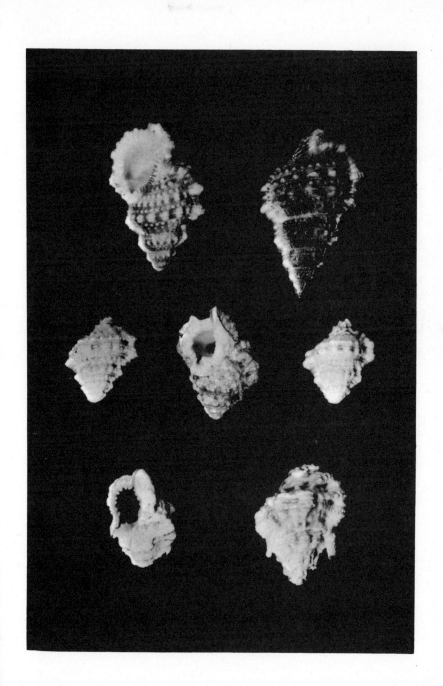

THE TUN SHELL FAMILY

FAMILY TONNIDAE (DOLIDIDAE)

The tun shells are a small group of less than thirty species which inhabit the Indo-Pacific area. They may be recognized by their large, thin, globular shell, their inflated body whorl and wide aperture, and their spiral ribs.

THE PARTRIDGE TUN SHELL   *Tonna perdix* (Linnaeus)

The partridge tun bears a shell which is large, thin, and hard; the body whorl is inflated and the aperture is very wide. The shell is brownish in color and is usually covered over the outer surface by a reticulated pattern of white lines. Shells are occasionally found, however, which have this reticulated pattern lacking over a part or all of the shell; this color variety is illustrated in the lower figures in the accompanying plate It ranges in length from two to six inches.

This species appears to be distributed over the entire world in warn water. It is found from the Hawaiian Islands southward through Poly nesia, then westward across the tropical Pacific Ocean, through the Eas Indies, and across the Indian Ocean to the coast of Africa. It likewis occurs in the West Indies and in the warm waters along the Atlantic coas of South America.

THE BLACK LIPPED TUN SHELL   *Tonna melanostoma* (Jay)

The black lipped tun shell is a thin, large, and heavily ribbed species with a large body whorl and a large aperture. It is colored by black, brown, yellow, and white markings which are arranged somewhat in longitudinal bands. The columella and the outer lip are marked with black. It is a large species with a shell ranging in size from two to at least nine inches in length.

This is an Indo-Pacific species extending from the Hawaiian Islands southward through Polynesia and westward across the entire tropical Pacific Ocean.

Center

THE CHANNELLED TUN SHELL   *Tonna canaliculata* (Linnaeus)

The shell of this species is large, thin, and hard, with a large body whorl and a large aperture. The suture is characteristically depressed and is the feature from which the shell derives its name. It varies in length from two to five inches.

This is an Indo-Pacific species which extends from the Hawaiian Islands southward and westward through all of the islands of the tropical Pacific Ocean to the Philippine Islands, through the East Indies, and across the Indian Ocean.

THE SPOTTED TUN SHELL   *Tonna dolium* (Linnaeus)

This tun shell is a beautiful species with a large thin shell and an inflated body whorl. It is white and bluish white in color and is spotted with brown upon the ridges. It ranges from two to six inches in length.

This mollusc extends from the Hawaiian Islands southward and westward across the entire tropical Pacific Ocean, through the East Indies, and across the Indian Ocean to the coast of Africa.

Center and Lower Row

THE APPLE TUN SHELL   *Malea pomum* (Linnaeus)

The shell of the apple tun is thicker than that of other species and bears teeth upon the lips. It is white and amber in color and ranges in length from two to three inches.

This species extends from the Hawaiian Islands southward through Polynesia and westward across the tropical Pacific Ocean to the Philippine Islands, through the East Indies, and across the tropical Indian Ocean to the coast of Africa.

THE ROCK SHELL FAMILY

FAMILY MURICIDAE

The rock shells are a miscellaneous assemblage of variously shaped shells. They are in general thick, heavy, solid shells of spiral design in which the whorls are usually covered by varices, nodules, or spines, all of which add to the weight and thickness of the shell. The apertures are usually roundish in outline, are covered by a horny operculum, and terminate in a straight anterior canal or notch.

The members of this group are active and carnivorous in their habits and are most commonly found in shallow water in rocky areas. They are a large group which occur in all of the oceans of the world, but are most numerous in the tropics.

THE FRANCOLIN ROCK SHELL *Nassa francolinus* (Bruguiere)

This mollusc produces a shell which is firm and heavy in construction. The outside of this shell is usually smooth although it may exhibit fine striations in some specimens. It is variously colored with white, cream, yellow, brown, and sometimes purple. It is further marked about the center with an irregular row of somewhat triangular areas. It will reach a length of two and one-half inches.

This species is distributed from the Hawaiian Islands southward through Polynesia, then westward across the entire tropical Pacific Ocean, through the many islands of the East Indies, and across the Indian Ocean to the Red Sea.

This species is most commonly found in books under the name of *Nassa sertum* (Bruguiere).

Upper Row, Right and Left; Lower Row

THE YELLOW MOUTHED DRUPE   *Drupa ochrostoma* (Bl.) v. *spectrum* (R.)

This shell is encircled by fine ridges and is marked longitudinally by furrows and ridges bearing nodules. It is pure white over the entire outer surface; the aperture may vary in color from white to orange. It will reach a length of about one and one-half inches.

This species is distributed from the Hawaiian Islands southward and westward through Polynesia, through the entire tropical Pacific Ocean to the Philippine Islands, and through the East Indies.

Upper Row, Center

THE PURPLE MOUTHED DRUPE SHELL   *Drupa porphyrostoma* (Reeve)

This species has a shell which is grooved longitudinally and encircled by many fine ridges. It is yellow or white in color without and is usually a blue or violet color within the aperture. It will reach a length of nearly one inch. This mollusc is distributed from the Hawaiian Islands southward into Polynesia.

Second Row

THE KNOBBED DRUPE SHELL   *Drupa nodus* (St. Vincent)

The surface of this species is covered with rows of tubercles which are separated by a single spiral ridge. The shell is white or orange in color, the tubercles are black, and the aperture is violet. It will reach a length of one inch.

This species is distributed from the Hawaiian Islands southward to Polynesia and possibly elsewhere in the Indo-Pacific area.

Third Row, Left Pair

THE BROWN LIPPED DRUPE SHELL   *Drupa brunneolabrum* (Dall)

The shell of this species is rough externally and is crossed by small transverse ridges and by rough folds. The tubercles which cover the body whorl are larger posteriorly. It will reach about one inch in length.

This species is found in Hawaiian waters and possibly elsewhere in the Pacific area. It is found in some collections under the name of *Purpura foliacea* Conrad.

Third Row, Right Pair

THE GRANULAR DRUPE SHELL   *Drupa granulata* (Duclos)

The surface of this species is covered by very fine revolving ridges and spiral rows of tubercles. The shell is dark brown or black in color. The aperture is lighter in color, usually violet or blue, and is bordered by two large and two smaller teeth. It will reach one inch in length.

This species is distributed from the Hawaiian Islands southward and westward through the warm waters of the tropical Pacific Ocean to Japan and the Philippine Islands.

THE LITTLE BASKET DRUPE SHELL   *Drupa fiscellum* (Gmelin)

The surface of this species is longitudinally and spirally ridged forming a reticulated pattern with deep pits. The aperture is purplish and bears whitish teeth within. It measures about three-fourths of an inch in length.

The specimen shown on the accompanying plate is from the Hawaiian Islands.

The name of *Morula mitosa* is used by some to designate this species.

Second Row

THE BUSHY DRUPE SHELL   *Drupa* species

The surface of this shell is longitudinally ridged and grooved. A row of spots placed in the grooves form an interrupted brown band which encircles the body whorl. The shell is brownish white without and purplish-gray within the inner lip. It will reach a length of about three-fourths of an inch. This species is believed to be *Drupa dumosa* (Conrad). It resembles *Drupa ochrostoma* somewhat, but it differs from it in the color of the mouth.

Third Row

THE SMALL DRUPE SHELL   *Drupa parva* (Reeve)

This morula is crossed by longitudinal and transverse ridges which bear nodules. The spire is sharp and the aperture is small. It is whitish in color and the nodules are in alternate rows of orange and black. It measures about one-half inch in length.

This species is distributed from the Hawaiian Islands southward and westward through the warm waters of the Pacific Ocean at least as far as the Philippine Islands.

Fourth Row

THE BROWN SCALY DRUPE SHELL   *Drupa fuscoimbricata* (Sowerby)

This morula is oval or spindle shaped and is covered with sharp, conical tubercles. In life the shell is reddish brown in color; in old shells it is white with red tubercles. It will reach a length of about one inch.

This species is found in the Hawaiian Islands and possibly elsewhere in the Pacific Ocean.

Lower Row

THE YELLOW MOUTHED DRUPE SHELL   *Drupa ochrostoma* (Blainville)

This morula is marked by longitudinal grooves and ridges which bear prominent tubercles where they cross smaller encircling ridges. It varies in color from white through yellowish to chocolate; the aperture may be either white or yellowish in color. It is about one inch in length.

This species is found from the Hawaiian Islands southward throughout Polynesia, westward across the entire tropical Pacific to the Philippine Islands, and through the islands of the East Indies.

Many collectors regard *Drupa spectrum* (Reeve) and *Drupa elata* (Blainville) as varieties of this species.

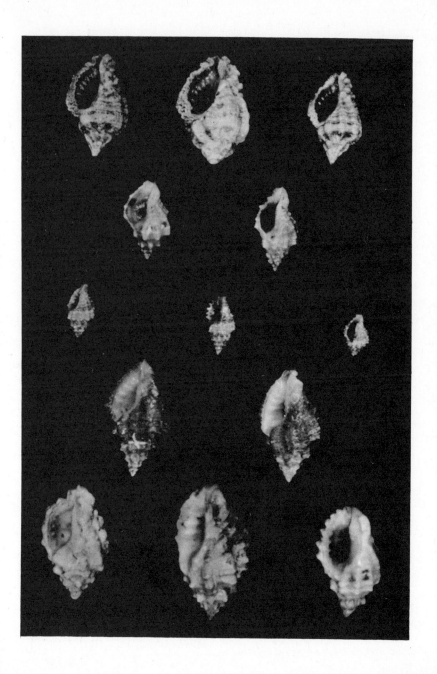

Upper Row; Upper Center

THE MULBERRY DRUPE SHELL *Drupa morum* Röding

The shell of this mollusc is extremely heavy and thick and is covered over the outer surface by large, heavy, blunt tubercles. The spire is very short and the aperture is toothed on both sides. The outside of the shell is a dirty whitish color with black upon the tubercles. The aperture is violet. Large specimens will measure one and three-fourths or possibly two inches in length.

This species is distributed from the Hawaiian Islands southward and westward across the entire tropical Pacific Ocean to the Philippine Islands.

Lower Center; Lower Row

THE SHOWY OR BRILLIANT DRUPE SHELL *Drupa speciosa* (Dunker)

This mollusc has a heavy shell which is encircled by very fine ridges. It is also grooved and ridged longitudinally with large tubercles placed upon the ridges. Both the outer lip and the columella are toothed. The outer surface is yellowish white in color, while the aperture is rose colored within and is bordered about the lip by yellow or yellowish brown. It varies in length from one and one-half to two and one-half inches.

This species is distributed from the Hawaiian Islands southward throughout Polynesia.

Some individuals regard this mollusc as a variety of *Drupa rubus-caesius* Röding.

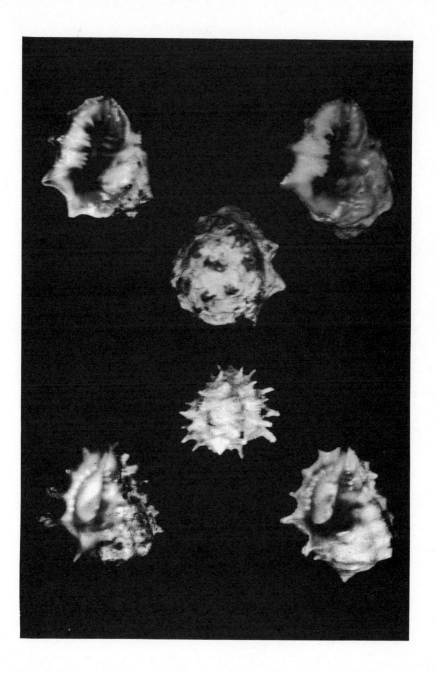

THE GOOSEBERRY DRUPE SHELL   *Drupa grossularia* Röding

This drupe shell is compressed in form and has a short spire. The outer surface is covered by very small scales and by low spiral ridges. These ridges become knobby toward the spire and are drawn out beyond the lip to form finger-like processes. The outer surface is whitish or yellowish in color, while the aperture is a bright orange or yellow color. It will reach one and one-half inches in length.

This species is found from the Hawaiian Islands southward and westward throughout the central tropical Pacific Ocean.

Middle Row

THE CASTOR BEAN DRUPE   *Drupa ricina* (Linnaeus)

This mollusc produces a shell which is low and dome-like in appearance and covered by short black-tipped spines. A well developed row of spines borders the outer lip. The aperture is bordered by teeth on both the outer and inner margins. The shell is white in color, both outside and inside, except for the spines which are black tipped.

The distribution of this species extends from the Hawaiian Islands southward throughout Polynesia, along New Zealand, across the entire tropical Pacific Ocean to Japan, through the East Indies, and across the Indian Ocean to the Red Sea.

Lower Row

THE SPIDER-LIKE DRUPE   *Drupa arachnoides* (Lamarck)

This drupe shell is low and dome-like in appearance and is covered over the upper surface by black tipped spines which become longer toward the margin. The inner and outer sides of the aperture are bordered by teeth. It is white in color over the outer surface except for the spines which are marked with black. The aperture is bordered by yellow or orange. It is about one inch in length.

This species is distributed from the Hawaiian Islands southward throughout Polynesia and westward through the warm waters of the tropical Pacific Ocean.

Some individuals regard this species as a variety of *Drupa ricina* (Linnaeus).

This dye shell is a large and interesting species with a straight, thick, heavy, spindle-shaped shell which ends in a pointed spire. It is covered over the outer surface by two rows of large, heavy, blunt tubercles between which spiral striations are often visible. The aperture is comparatively small in this species and the outer lip is toothed on its inner margin. The entire outer surface of the shell is white in color and the aperture is a yellowish brown color within. It will reach a length of at least three inches.

This species is distributed from the Hawaiian Islands southward through Polynesia and the tropical Pacific Ocean.

This species is often confused with *Purpura armigera* (Link).

THE INTERMEDIATE DYE SHELL   *Purpura intermedia* Kiener

This shell is heavy and firm in construction, low and domelike in outline, and is covered over the outer surface with low, blunt tubercles. It is yellowish white and brownish in color and is marked over the columella and outer lip with brown; the aperture is bluish within. It is about one and one-half inches in length.

This species is found from the Hawaiian Islands southward and westward across the entire tropical Pacific and Indian Oceans.

Middle Row

THE HARP DYE SHELL   *Purpura harpa* (Conrad)

The shell of this mollusc is covered by revolving ridges which are crossed by oblique longitudinal furrows and ridges. The outer surface of the shell is chocolate in color and spotted with white; the shell is bluish within and is marked with brown upon the lip and on the columella. It will reach a length of about one and one-fourth inches.

This species is known from the Hawaiian Islands and probably elsewhere in the Pacific area.

Lower Row

THE OPEN DYE SHELL   *Purpura aperta* (Blainville)

This mollusc produces a shell which is large, heavy, and dome-shaped and which is covered with short blunt tubercles or spines. It is white or yellowish in color on the outside of the shell; the aperture is white within but is tinged with yellow about the lip and on the columella. It will reach three inches in length.

This species occurs in the Hawaiian Islands and probably elsewhere in the Pacific area.

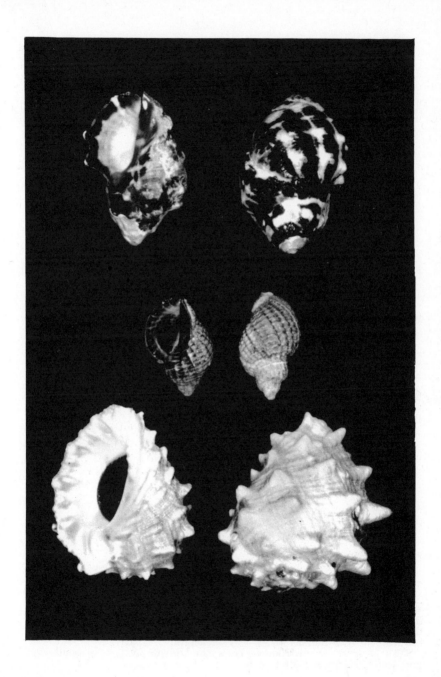

Upper Row

THE LONG DRUPE SHELL   *Drupa serrialis longus* (Pils. and Van.)

This shell resembles a triton in appearance and was long grouped with that family. The spire is well developed and the body is marked by a network of longitudinal and spiral ribs on which tubercles may occur. It is yellowish and white in color and the tubercles, when present, are usually white with black tips. Older specimens tend to be lighter in color and smoother on the outer surface. It will reach a length of about one inch.

This species is distributed from the Hawaiian Islands southward throughout Polyneia, across the entire tropical Pacific Ocean, through the East Indies, and across the Indian Ocean to the Red Sea.

Second Row

THE MANY COLORED SHELL   *Pinaxia versicolor* (Gray)

This mollusc bears a shell which is shaped somewhat like the cone shells. It has a short spire, a large aperture, and often bears tubercles on the shoulder of the body whorl. In older specimens the columella may bear plications. It varies in color from whitish to brownish and is encircled by brown bands; the aperture is yellowish within. It is about three-fourths of an inch in length.

This species is distributed from the Hawaiian Islands southward throughout Polynesia, across the entire tropical Pacific Ocean, through the East Indies, and across the Indian Ocean.

This species is sometimes found in collections under the name of *Pinaxia coronata* A. Adams.

Third Row

THE TWO EDGED SHELL   *Aspella anceps* (Lamarck)

Two varices placed upon opposite sides of the shell divide this shell into two halves and give it an arrow-headed apperance. The surface of the shell is folded between the varices and is encircled by fine lines. It has a short, recurved canal and a round aperture. It is white in color and will reach a length of about an inch.

This species is distributed from the Hawaiian Islands southward throughout Polynesia, along the coast of Australia and westward across the entire tropical Pacific Ocean to Japan; it also is reported to occur in the West Indies and Panama.

This shell is often found in the Genus *Ranella* Lamarck within the family of the tritons (Cymatiidae).

Lower Row, Right and Left

THE HAWAIIAN ROCK SHELL   *Vitularia sandwichensis* (Pease)

The shell of this species is small, somewhat bulbous, spindle-shaped, and has the body whorl sharply angled at the shoulder. The outer surface is marked by six wrinkled, oblique varices and the aperture is toothed on the inner margin of the outer lip. It is white in color within and without. It will reach a length of at least one inch.

This species is known from the Hawaiian Islands and probably elsewhere in the Pacific area.

Lower Row, Center Pair

THE DARK BROWN DRUPE SHELL   *Drupa fusconigra* (Pease)

This is a spindle shaped species in which the whorls are marked by encircling granular ribs and fine longitudinal wrinkles. The exterior of the shell is brownish to black in color, the lips are purplish to brown, and the teeth within the outer lip range from white to bluish. It varies from one-half to three-fourths of an inch in length.

This mollusc is distributed from the Hawaiian Islands southward through Polynesia and Melanesia.

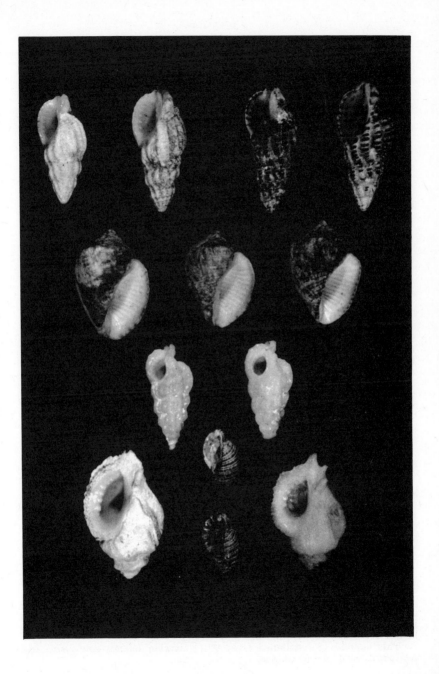

THE CORAL LOVING SHELL FAMILY

FAMILY RAPIDAE (CORALLIOPHILIDAE)

The shells within this family are mostly bulbous forms with encircling ribs. They make their home in shallow water and are most often found in crevices, in porous coral rock, or in colonies of living coral.

These molluscs are related to the Muricidae and are sometimes placed within that family.

Upper Row

CORAL SHELL *Rhizochilus madreporarum* (Sowerby)

This low, dome-shaped shell is oval in outline and possesses a very wide aperture. The surface of the shell is rough and is marked with many fine transverse striae. The spire is small and usually not apparent. The outer surface of the shell is white in color while the interior is purple or violet. It ranges in length from one-half to one and one-fourth inches.

This species extends from the Hawaiian Islands southward and westward through Polynesia, across the entire tropical Pacific Ocean to Japan, through the East Indies, and across the Indian Ocean.

Second Row

LAMARCK'S CORAL SHELL *Leptoconchus lamarckii* Deshayes

The shell of this species is elongated, somewhat spindle shaped, and is composed of about three striated whorls in which the sutures are concealed. The columella is arched and elongated and is bordered by an oblique aperture.

These molluscs are found imbedded in coral or coralline rocks.

This species is found from the Hawaiian Islands southward and westward across the entire tropical Pacific and Indian Oceans.

Third Row

THE DEFORMED CORAL SHELL *Coralliophila deformis* (Lamarck)

This species is a short, bulbous form with a small, sharp spire and a very wide aperture. It is spirally striated without and exhibits some longitudinal sculpture. It is whitish on the outside and somewhat reddish within the aperture. It measures from one to one and one-half inches.

This mollusc is distributed from the Hawaiian Islands southward and westward through the tropical Pacific Ocean.

Fourth Row

THE BULB-SHAPED CORAL SHELL *Coralliophila bulbiformis* (Sowerby)

This mollusc bears a shell which is short and bulbous in form and a spire which is comparatively longer than that of *C. neretoidea*. The outer surface is marked by spiral ridges and by longitudinal furrows. The aperture is striated within and the outer lip is wrinkled. The color of the shell is whitish on the outside and rose colored within the aperture. It ranges in length from three-fourths to one and one-fourth inches.

This mollusc is found from the Hawaiian Islands southward and westward through Polynesia and the warm waters of the tropical Pacific Ocean.

Lower Row

THE NERITA-LIKE CORAL SHELL *Coralliophila violacea* (Kiener)

The shell of this species is swollen and bulbous in outline and bears a spire which is comparatively longer than that of *C. violacea*. The It is white in color without and purplish within the aperture. It ranges in length from one to one and one-half inches.

This mollusc is distributed from the Hawaiian Islands southward and westward through the tropical Pacific Ocean.

124

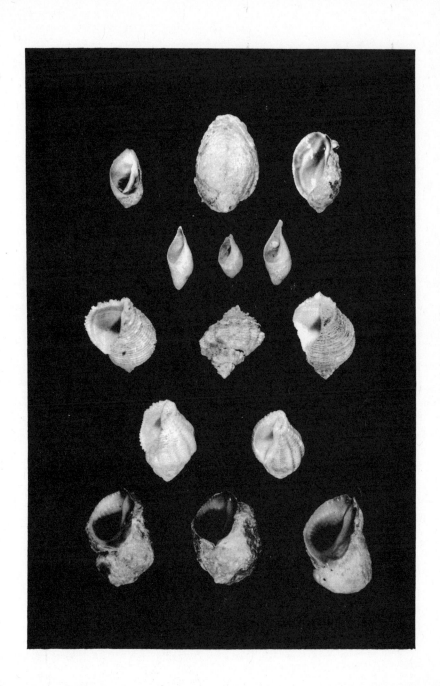

THE LITTLE DOVE SHELL FAMILY
FAMILY PYRENIDAE (COLUMBELLIDAE)

The little dove shells are a group of small, solid species with protruding spires. They vary greatly in shape and include shells which are triangular, spindle shaped, and ellipsoid in outline. The anterior canal is short and the columella is arched and tuberculated below. The outer lip is thickened, curved at the middle, and toothed on the inner border. A horny operculum is present and an epidermis covers the shell.

Upper Row

THE LINED LITTLE DOVE SHELL   *Columbella lineolata* Kiener

This is a variable species in which the whorls are longitudinally ribbed. It is white in color or is marked with brown spots. It measures from one-half to two-thirds of an inch in length.

This species is found in the Hawaiian Islands and elsewhere in the Pacific area.

Some individuals regard this species as identical to *Columbella terpsichore* Sowerby from the West Indies.

Second Row

THE MOLECULAR LITTLE DOVE SHELL   *Pyrene moleculina* (Duclos)

This little shell is of uncertain identity. It is white in color and is marked with brown.

This shell is found in the Hawaiian Islands and possibly elsewhere in the Pacific area.

Third Row

THE ZEBRA LITTLE DOVE SHELL   *Columbella zebra* Gray

This little dove shell is somewhat spindle shaped and has a spire which is larger than most members of this group. The body whorl may be smooth or may have the posterior portion of it longitudinally folded, but it is nearly always spirally striated at the anterior end. The aperture is broad and the lip is slightly thickened and feebly toothed within. It is white in color and is marked longitudinally with zig-zag, zebra-like, brownish markings; the aperture is faintly violet within. It will reach a length of about one-half inch.

This species extends from the Hawaiian Islands southward through Polynesia to New Zealand and westward through the warm waters of the Pacific Ocean to Japan.

Fourth Row

THE TURTLE DOVE SHELL *Columbella turturina* Lamarck

This dove shell is short and thick and has an enlarged and swollen body whorl. It is white in color and is often marked with yellowish-brown. It will reach about two-thirds of an inch in length.

This species is distributed from the Hawaiian Islands southward and westward through the tropical Pacific Ocean to the Philippine Islands and the islands of the East Indies.

Fifth Row

LITTLE DOVE SHELL *Columbella* species

This dove shell represents an unidentified species from the Hawaiian Islands.

Sixth Row

THE PRETTY LITTLE DOVE SHELL *Pyrene bella* (Reeve)

This dove shell is spindle shaped and has a long pointed spire. It is yellowish white in color and is marked by light brownish areas and spots. It measures about one-half inch in length.

This mollusc is distributed from the Hawaiian Islands southward and westward through all of the tropical waters of the Pacific Ocean to the coast of Asia.

THE VARIABLE LITTLE DOVE SHELL   *Columbella varians* Sowerby

This shell is somewhat oval in shape and has a short spire. The exterior surface is usually smooth, although it is often spirally grooved and bears longitudinal ribs in varying degrees of prominence. The aperture is narrowed posteriorly and the outer lip is angled and toothed within.

This species is white in color with variable markings. It may range from almost pure white to nearly pure brown, but it is usually marked with interrupted brown bands. The columella is always brown tipped and the aperture is white within. It ranges in length from one-fourth to one-half inch.

This mollusc is distributed from the Hawaiian Islands southward and westward through the warm tropical Pacific Ocean to the Philippine Islands and the islands of the East Indies. It has also been reported from the Galapagos Islands.

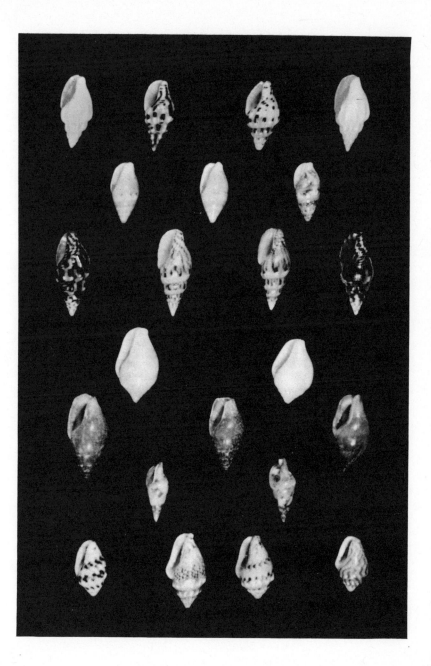

THE WHELK SHELL FAMILY

FAMILY BUCCINIDAE

The whelks are large, thick, oblong or spindle-shaped shells with few body whorls and with large apertures which are usually terminated in a notch in front. The outer lip is simple, though often thickened, and the columella is without folds. The operculum which closes the aperture is horny in composition. The whole outside of the shell is covered by a thick periostracum. The members of this family are a carnivorous, aggressive lot and are distributed from the warm waters of the tropics nearly to the poles.

Upper and Middle Rows

THE TRITON-LIKE WHELK   *Pisania tritonoides* (Reeve)

This mollusc bears a shell which in many ways resembles the shells of the tritons. It is spiral in design and has a smooth external surface marked by many fine encircling lines. The shell is variously colored with yellowish, whitish, and reddish brown areas. It will reach a length of about one and one-half inches.

This species is distributed from the Hawaiian Islands southward and westward across the entire tropical Pacific Ocean, through the East Indies, and across the Indian Ocean to the coast of Africa.

Some authorities regard this species as a variety of a widely distributed Indo-Pacific form known as *Pisania ignea* (Gmelin).

Lower Row

THE MARBLED WHELK   *Engina billeheusti* (Petit)

This shell like the previous one is somewhat triton-like in general appearance. The entire outer surface is covered by a network of longitudinal ribs crossed by revolving ribs. It is whitish in color, marked with reddish or brownish spots and areas, and will reach a length of about one and one-half inches.

This is a Pacific species extending from the Hawaiian Islands southward and westward to Japan and the Philippine Islands.

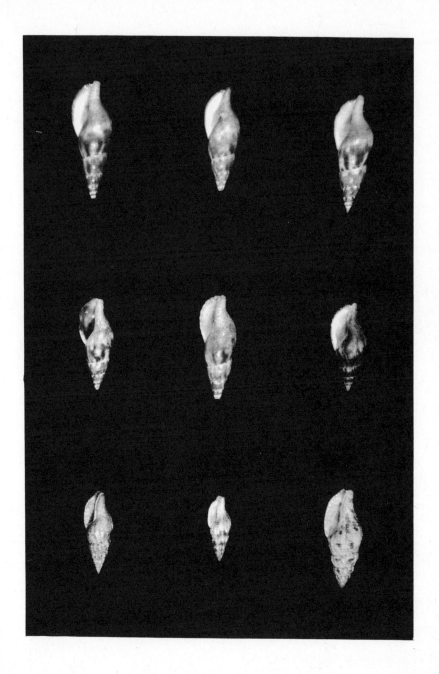

THE BASKET SHELL FAMILY

NASSARIIDAE (NASSIDAE; ALECTRIONIDAE)

The members of this group are all of small or moderate size and are usually of an oval or conical shape. The outer surface of these shells varies among the species. They may be ridged, covered with tubercles, smooth, or even polished, but they never have varices upon them. The inner lip of the shell is usually spread over the columella and the outer lip is thickened and usually bears teeth. These creatures are usually sand dwelling forms and burrow about in their search for bivalves and other molluscs on which to feed.

Upper Row, Right and Left

THE PIMPLED BASKET SHELL   Nassarius papillosus (Linnaeus)

This species is one of the larger members of this family. It is a sturdy shell, somewhat oval or conical in shape, and is covered by regularly spaced papillose tubercles. The outer lip is bordered by teeth. It is whitish in color and usually marked by yellowish brown blotches and often by a pink tip upon the spire; the aperture is white in color. It ranges in length from one and one-fourth to two and one-fourth inches.[1]

Upper Row, Center

THE SPLENDID BASKET SHELL   Nassarius splendidulus (Dunker)

The outer surface of this species is crossed by deep spiral lines and longitudinal ribs which give a granular appearance to the surface. The sutures between the whorls are also deeply incised. It is white in color with a shining surface which is often marked with light chestnut brown colors. It is a small species ranging from one-half to three-fourths of an inch in length.[2]

Middle Row

THE PAINTED BASKET SHELL   Nassarius reeveanus (Dunker)

This species is oval or conical in shape, with a rather small aperture, a sharp spire, a smooth and polished surface, an arched and calloused columella, and thickened lips. It is longitudinally ribbed, particularly upon the spire, and has the suture ornamented with small tubercles. It is also marked with encircling lines. It is white, yellow, and brown in color and will reach a length of about one inch.[3]

Lower Row

THE ROUGH BASKET SHELL   Nassarius hirta Kiener

This shell is oval or conical in shape and bears a sharp, turreted spire. The sutures are deep and are bordered by coronations along their anterior margin. The polished surface is longitudinally ribbed upon the spire and these ribs extend onto the body whorl in varying degrees of intensity. It is yellowish or orange brown in color and is often encircled with a paler central band; the aperture is white. It will reach a length of one inch.[4]

---

[1] This species is distributed from the Hawaiian Islands southward through Polynesia and westward as far as the Philippine Islands.

[2] This is a Pacific Ocean form extending from the Hawaiian Islands southward through Polynesia, westward across the tropical Pacific Ocean to the Philippine Islands, and through the many islands of the East Indies. This species is often found under the name of *Nassa ranida* A. Adams.

[3] It extends from the Hawaiian Islands southward through Polynesia, westward across the tropical Pacific Ocean to the Philippine Islands, through the East Indies, and across the entire Indian Ocean. It has also been reported from the Cape Verde Islands off the west coast of Africa. This species is often found under the name of *Nassarius graphiterus* (Beck) *or Alectrion pictus* (Dunker).

[4] This species is distributed from the Hawaiian Islands southward throughout Polynesia, along the coast of Australia, westward through the tropical Pacific Ocean to the Philippine Islands, through the East Indies, and into the Indian Ocean.

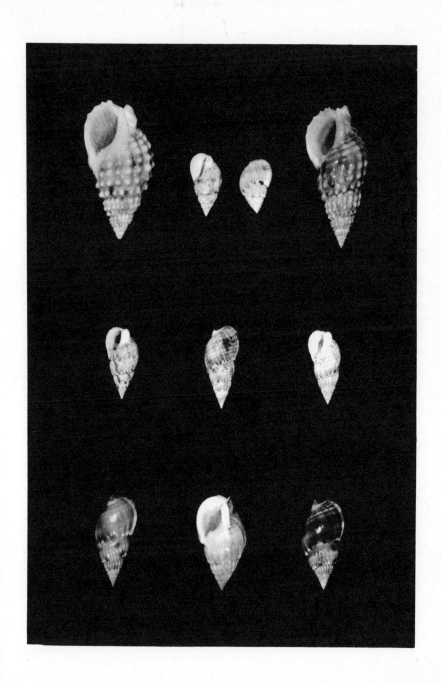

THE SPINDLE SHELL FAMILY

FAMILY FASCIOLARIIDAE

The spindle shells are usually strong, thick, and heavy, and as their name suggests spindle-like in shape. The spire of their shell is elevated, sharply pointed, and without varices. The outer lip is not thickened and the inner lip is usually marked by a few oblique plaits or plications. The operculum is ovate in outline and the columella lacks the umbilicus. The spindle shells are a group of slow moving, predatory animals which make their home in tropical seas.

Upper Row, Right and Left; Middle Row, Right and Left

THE HAWAIIAN SPINDLE SHELL   *Fusinus sandwichensis* (Sowerby)

This beautiful shell is spindle shaped and of spiral design with an extremely long anterior canal and spire. It is entirely white in color and in life is covered by a brown epidermis. It is usually between three and four inches in length.

This species is a central Pacific form occurring about the Hawaiian Islands at depths of four or five fathoms or more.

Center

THE WAVY SPINDLE SHELL   *Fusinus undatus* (Gmelin)

This species has a large, thick, heavy, spindle-shaped shell with a very long anterior canal and spire. The whorls are marked by large tubercles and the interior of the aperture is spirally ridged. The shell is white outside and inside. It ranges in length from five to seven inches.

This species extends from the Hawaiian Islands southward and westward through Polynesia and the warm tropical waters of the central and south Pacific Ocean.

Lower Row

THE KNOBBY SPINDLE SHELL   *Latirus nodus* Martin

The shell of this species is elongated and spindle-shaped with a long anterior canal and an elongated spire which is covered with low rounded tubercles. It varies in color from orange brown to light yellow. The aperture is rosy in color. It ranges from two and one-half to three and one-half inches in length.

This species is distributed from the Hawaiian Islands southward and westward through Polynesia, Melanesia, and the islands of the tropical Pacific Ocean.

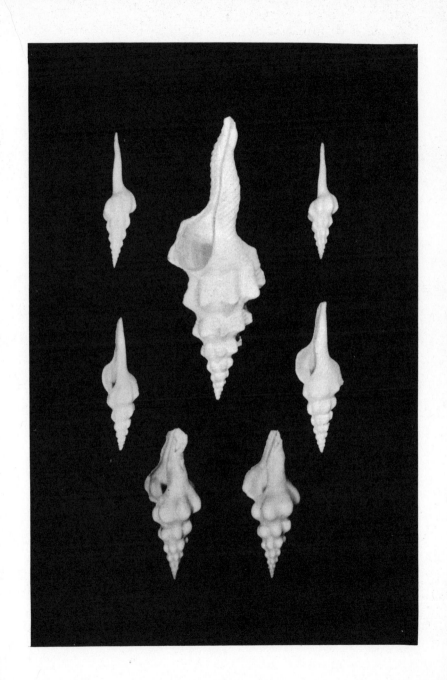

THE GREEN MOUTHED SPINDLE SHELL *Peristernia chlorostoma* Sowerby

This common little shell is spindle-shaped and short in form. It is furrowed longitudinally and marked by fine spiral ridges. The shell is yellowish green in color and marked with brown. It will reach a length of about three-fourths of an inch.

This species is distributed from the Hawaiian Islands southward and westward through all of the warm waters of the Pacific Ocean to New Zealand and the Philippine Islands, through the East Indies, and into the Indian Ocean.

THAANUM'S SPINDLE SHELL *Peristernia thaanumi* Pilsbry and Bryan

This species is spindle-shaped, short and robust in form, and is marked by shallow longitudinal furrows and spiral ridges. The outer lip is toothed. It is yellowish white or light yellow in color and will reach a length of three-fourths of an inch.

It is known from the Hawaiian Islands and possibly elsewhere in the Indo-Pacific area.

This little mollusc is named in honor of Mr. Ditlev Thaanum of Honolulu.

THE OLIVE SHELL FAMILY

Family Olividae

The olive or rice shells are usually quite cylindrical in shape, brightly colored, and are smooth and polished over the outside. These shells look somewhat like cones for they have a very large body whorl which conceals the early volutions of the shell; unlike the cones however they have no epidermis. The aperture is large and narrow and terminates anteriorly in an oblique notch. The outer lip is simple and the operculum is either missing or very small.

The olive shells are widely distributed in the warmer waters of the world.

The Hawaiian Olive Shell   *Oliva sandwichensis* Pease

This olive shell exhibits the characteristic shape of the members of its family. It is roughly cylindrical in shape with a smooth exterior surface and with a spire which is short and pointed. This shell varies widely in color, intensity, and pattern. It is usually yellowish white in color and is marked with chestnut brown blotches. The aperture is yellowish brown. It varies in length from one to one and one-fourth inches.

This species inhabits the Hawaiian Islands.

Some regard this shell as a variety of *Oliva duclosi* Reeve, a species which is distributed throughout Polynesia, along the coasts of Australia, New Zealand, and China, and through the Philippine Islands and the East Indies.

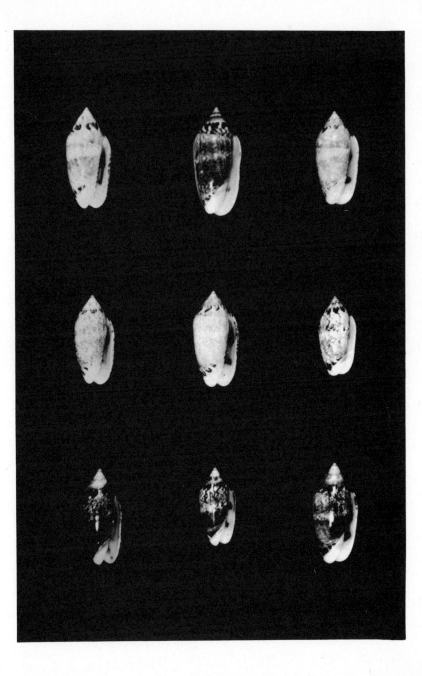

THE MITER SHELL FAMILY

Family Mitridae

The miter shells are usually thick, heavy, solid, spindle shaped shells with sharp tapering spires. The apertures of these shells are small, narrow, and notched in front. The outer lip is usually thin and is quite often toothed along its inner margin. The columella also bears several plaits or plications upon it. The epidermis is usually very thin or absent.

This family is limited to the warm seas of the world.

The Episcopal Miter Shell   *Mitra mitra* (Linnaeus)

This miter shell is a large, slender species with a smooth surface and an outer lip which is bordered by fine pointed teeth. It is white in color and is marked with somewhat rectangular red spots which are arranged in spiral rows. It will reach a length of nearly six inches.

This species is distributed from the Hawaiian Islands southward throughout Polynesia, westward across the Pacific Ocean to the Philippine Islands, through the East Indies, and across the tropical waters of the Indian Ocean.

For many years this species has been known as *Mitra episcopalis* (Linnaeus) and will be found in most books under this name.

THE PUNCTURED MITER SHELL   *Mitra stictica* (Link)

The shell of this species is fairly large and elongated and bears a long turreted spire. The surface of the shell is encircled by grooves bearing punctures; it is for this feature that the shell is named. The posterior edge of each whorl is marked by small folds or tubercles. The shell is yellowish white in color and will reach a length of at least two inches.

This species is found in the Hawaiian Islands and elsewhere in the Pacific area.

Lower Row

THE PAPAL MITER SHELL   *Mitra papalis* (Linnaeus)

This miter shell is a large species with a somewhat turreted spire. The posterior edge of each whorl is bordered by one row of tooth-like tubercles or folds; a few teeth also border the anterior edge of the outer lip. The shell is white in color and is marked with spiral rows of red spots and blotches. It will reach six inches in length.

This species is distributed from the Hawaiian Islands southward throughout Polynesia and westward across the tropical Pacific Ocean.

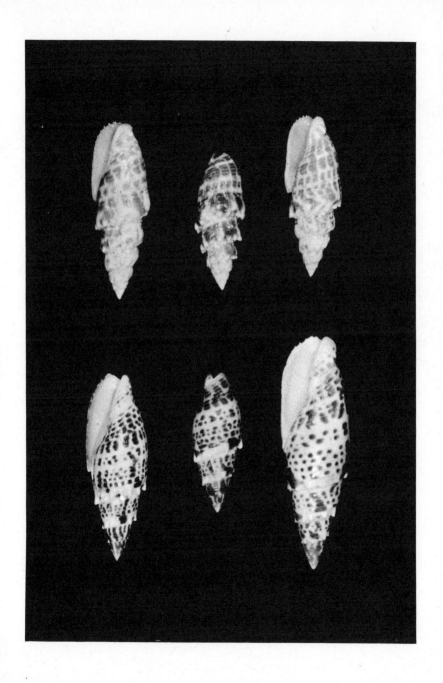

Upper Row

THE SHARP POINTED MITER SHELL   *Mitra exasperata* (Gmelin)

This miter shell is covered over the body whorl by longitudinal ridges and encircling grooves. The whorls are angulated about their posterior margin so as to give a turreted appearance to the spire. The columella bears four plaits and the aperture is striated within. This shell is·white to yellow in color and is marked with brown which is usually in the form of two bands, although the bands in some cases are restricted to the ridges. It will reach at least one inch in length.

This is an Indo-Pacific species extending from the Hawaiian Islands southward and westward throughout Polynesia, across the tropical Pacific Ocean to the Philippine Islands, through the East Indies, and across the Indian Ocean to the Red Sea.

Center Row

NEWCOMB'S MITER SHELL   *Mitra newcombii* Pease

Newcomb's miter shell is a rather elongated and spindle shaped species with a sharp pointed spire. It is marked by longitudinal grooves and by encircling grooves bearing punctures. The columella bears five plaits. This shell is white in color, encircled by a broad brown band, and marked with small reddish or brownish dots. It will reach a length of more than one inch.

Newcomb's miter is known from the Hawaiian Islands and probably elsewhere in the tropical Pacific Ocean.

Lower Row

THE PITTED MITER SHELL   *Mitra foveolata* Dunker

This miter shell is a slender spindle-shaped species with a turreted spire and is marked over the outer surface by longitudinal ribs and encircling ridges. It is white in color and is marked with orange-brown. It will reach at least one inch in length.

This is an Indo-Pacific species of puzzling identity. Some individuals believe it to be identical to *Mitra flammea* (Q. and G.), a Pacific species distributed from the Hawaiian Islands southward and westward throughout Polynesia and across the tropical Pacific Ocean to the coast of Asia.

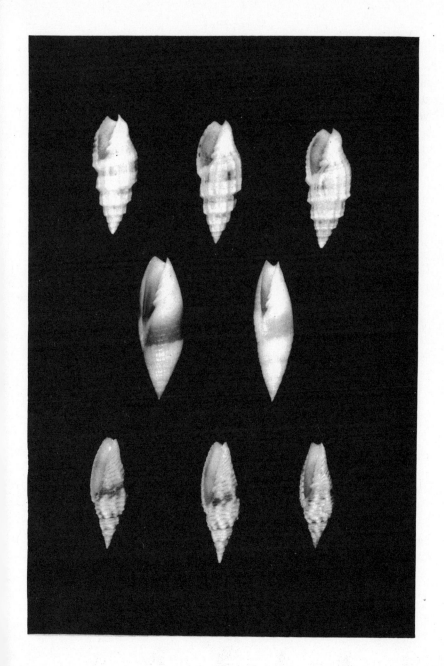

THE LACED OR UNBOUND MITER SHELL   *Mitra astricta* Lamarck

This miter shell has a fairly smooth surface which is marked by many fine longitudinal grooves and by spiral grooves which are brownish in color. The shell is usually almost white although it may be marked by yellow or brown colors. It will reach a length of about one and one-half inches.

This species is known from the Hawaiian Islands.

THE WHITE WASHED MITER SHELL   *Mitra dealbata* A. Adams

This mollusc bears a medium sized shell which is marked with four plaits upon the columella and by ridges upon the inner surface of the outer lip. The outer surface of the shell is smooth, but is crossed by a fine network of longitudinal and transverse grooves. It is white in color outside and inside and will reach a length of at least one and one-half inches.

This is a species of puzzling identity from the Hawaiian Islands. This and the preceding species may intergrade.

THE LETTERED MITER SHELL   *Mitra litterata* Lamarck

This common species has a shell which is stout in shape, thick and heavy in construction, and very nearly smooth upon the outside. The color varies considerably, but the pattern is usually one of brown markings upon a white shell. In some individuals the shell is nearly all brown and the white is reduced to a minimum. It will reach one inch in length.

This is an Indo-Pacific species which is distributed from the Hawaiian Islands southward throughout Polynesia, westward across the tropical Pacific Ocean to the Philippine Islands, through the East Indies, and across the Indian Ocean to the coast of Africa.

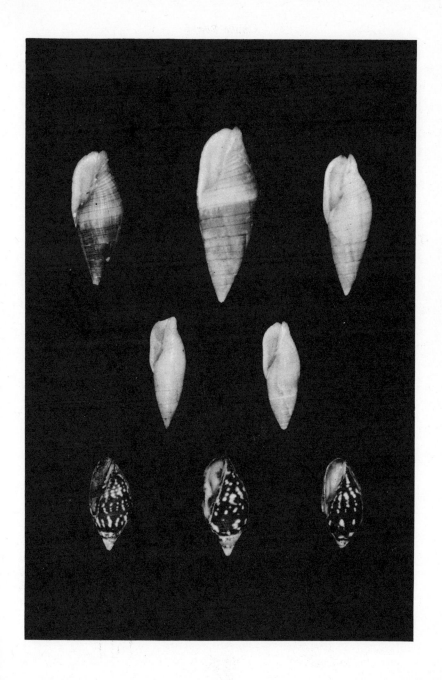

THE OLIVE-SHAPED MITER SHELL   *Mitra olivaeformis* Swainson

A somewhat cylindrical form gives this species a superficial resemblance to the olive shells. Its spire, although sharp and pointed, is relatively much shorter than in typical members of this group. It is yellowish orange in color over most of the outer surface with the exception of the anterior end which is usually marked with violet. It will reach a length of more than one-half inch.

This species is found from the Hawaiian Islands southward through Polynesia and probably elsewhere in the Pacific area.

Middle Row

THE THREAD LINED MITER SHELL   *Mitra filistriata* Sowerby

This mollusc has a rather slender shell with a long, slender, turreted and pointed spire. It is covered by a network of longitudinal and spiral grooves so that it has a rather rough surface. The color is usually yellow marked with brown areas. It will reach about one inch in length.

This species occurs in the Hawaiian Islands and probably elsewhere in the Pacific area.

Lower Row

THE BROWN MITER SHELL   *Mitra brunnea* Pease

This mollusc has a shell which is small, fairly stout and heavy in construction, and without distinctive external markings. The entire outer surface is yellowish brown in color and the aperture is white. It will reach one inch in length.

This species occurs in the Hawaiian Islands, throughout Polynesia, and probably elsewhere in the Pacific area.

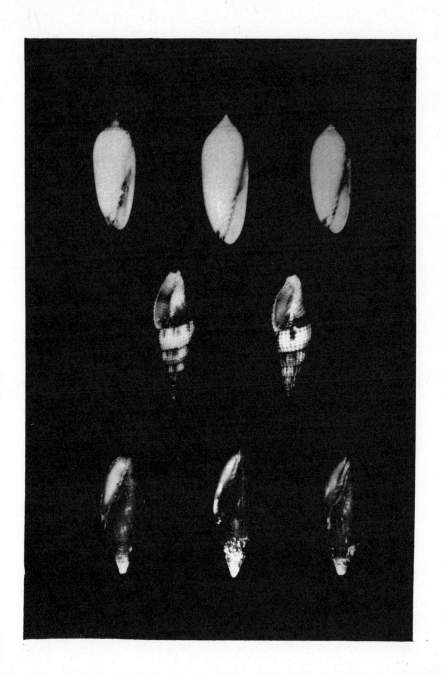

Upper Row, Right and Left

THE TICAO ISLAND MITER SHELL   *Mitra ticaonica* Reeve

The Ticao miter shell is an oval, thick, stocky species with a short spire. It has a rather smooth external surface marked by quite deep sutures and encircled by fine grooves. The columella bears four plaits. It is brown in color externally, purple within the aperture, and has the columellar plaits tipped with white. It measures about one inch in length.

This species extends from the Hawaiian Islands southward and westward to the Philippine Islands. A Hawaiian form in which the spire is less deeply grooved and the last whorl smoother has been named *Mitra ticaonica* Reeve variety *vagans* Pilsbry.

Upper Row, Center; Third Row, Center

THE KINDRED MITER SHELL   *Pusia consanguinea* (Reeve)

This small miter shell is marked with heavy longitudinal ridges which are crossed by many fine spiral lines. The columella bears four plaits. It is reddish in color and is marked by interrupted bands of white spots about the middle of the shell. It will reach three-fourths of an inch in length.

This species is distributed from the Hawaiian Islands southward and westward; it may possibly extend across the entire Indo-Pacific area.

Second Row

THE NODOSE MITER SHELL   *Mitra nodosa* Swainson

This miter shell is small in size, bears a turreted spire, and is covered over the entire outer surface by white nodules. The columella bears four plaits of which the posterior one is by far the largest. It is usually white in color but is sometimes marked by spots and bands of brown about the middle of the shell; the aperture is often yellowish within. It will reach three-fourths of an inch in length.

This species is distributed from the Hawaiian Islands southward throughout Polynesia, across the Pacific Ocean to the Philippine Islands and the coast of China, through the East Indies, and across the Indian Ocean to the Red Sea and the coast of Africa.

Third Row, Right and Left

THE BALDWIN MITER SHELL   *Mitra baldwini* Melvill

Baldwin's miter shell has the surface marked by fine revolving lines, the sutures of the spire slightly turreted, and the outer lip striated within. The shell has a brownish color pattern in life consisting of dark brown lines on a light brown background. The whorls are marked with longitudinal brown flame-like markings which are sometimes discontinuous on the body whorl. It will reach seven-eights of an inch in length.

This species was described from the Hawaiian Islands and was named for Mr. D. D. Baldwin, for many years principal of Haiku school on Maui.

Fourth Row

THE CUCUMBER MITER SHELL   *Mitra cucumerina* Lamarck

This mollusc bears a short, stocky, spindle-shaped shell which is encircled by grooves. It likewise bears teeth upon the outer lip. It is reddish orange in color and is often marked about the center with a band of white spots or lines. It will reach one and one-fourth inches in length.

It is distributed from the Hawaiian Islands southward throughout Polynesia and probably elsewhere in the Pacific area.

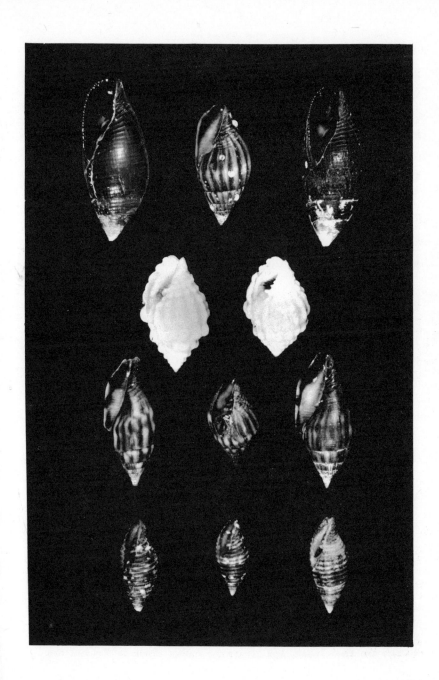

Upper Row

THE RUSTY MITER SHELL   *Mitra ferruginea* Lamarck

The rusty miter shell is a medium sized species with a tapering sharp pointed spire and with many parallel encircling ridges. The outer lip is crenated. It is white to yellowish in color and is longitudinally streaked with brown markings. It will reach a length of two and one-half inches.

This species is distributed from the Hawaiian Islands southward throughout Polynesia, across the Pacific Ocean to the Philippine Islands, through the East Indies, and into the Indian Ocean.

Middle Row

THE AMBIGUOUS MITER SHELL   *Mitra ambigua* Swainson

This is a large spindle-shaped species with a well developed, uniformly tapering spire. The outer surface is encircled by fine revolving grooves with punctures and the outer lip is edged with a row of fine teeth. It is orange brown in color and often exhibits a faint white band. It will reach two and one-half inches in length.

This species is distributed from the Hawaiian Islands southward and westward across the entire tropical Pacific Ocean to the Philippine Islands.

Lower Row, Left

THE ACUMINATED MITER SHELL   *Mitra acuminata* Swainson

This miter shell is somewhat oval in shape, of thick solid construction, and bears a well developed pointed spire. The shell is smooth over the outer surface and is marked posteriorly by a few fine encircling lines. The outer lip is thickened and the columella bears four plaits. It is of a yellowish color and may be covered by an epidermis in life. It will reach a length of one inch.

This species extends from the Hawaiian Islands southward throughout Polynesia and westward across the entire tropical Pacific Ocean to the Philippine Islands.

Lower Row, Center

LAMARCK'S MITER SHELL   *Mitra lamarcki* Deshayes

This miter shell is a rather slender species. It is white in color and is marked over the outer surface with light brown spots. It will reach a length of about two inches.

This mollusc is known from the Hawaiian Islands.

Lower Row, Right

THE CORONATED MITER SHELL   *Mitra coronata* Lamarck

This mollusc bears a shell with a comparatively smooth surface which is marked by spiral grooves bearing punctures and by a row of white tipped tubercles at the sutures. It is olive brown to light reddish brown in color and is usually marked with a white or yellowish band anterior to each suture. It will reach a length of one and three-fourths inches.

This species is distributed from the Hawaiian Islands southward and westward across the entire tropical Pacific Ocean to the Philippine Islands, through the East Indies, and across the Indian Ocean to the Red Sea.

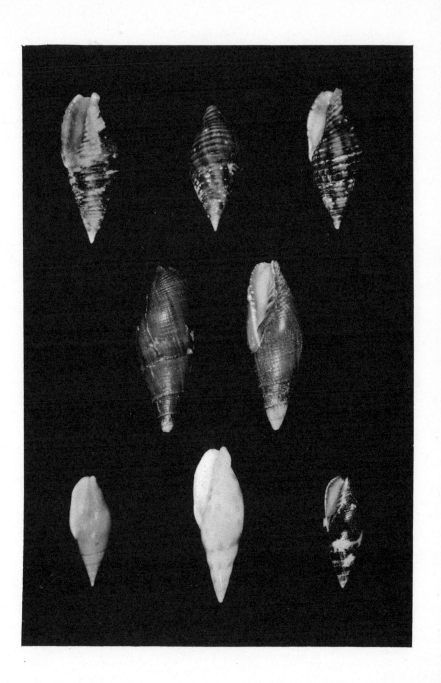

THE AURICLE-LIKE MITER SHELL   *Mitra auriculoides* Reeve

This miter shell is a stout, heavy, spindle-shaped species which is marked by five encircling punctured grooves upon an otherwise smooth surface. It is reddish brown or chocolate in color and bears a white or yellowish band which encircles the posterior part of the body whorl and ascends the spire. It will reach one inch in length.

This species is found in the Hawaiian Islands and throughout Polynesia.

MISCELLANEOUS MITER SHELLS   *Mitra* species

The shells figured in this rows are all species of uncertain identity from the Hawaiian Islands.

THE GOLDEN MITER SHELL   *Mitra aureolata* Swainson

This miter shell is a stout, spindle-shaped species which is marked by longitudinal folds and by encircling ribs. It is a variable species and shows considerable diversity in its sculpture, color, and markings. It ranges in color from brown through orange brown, orange, and lemon yellow to white; it is usually encircled by bands of a darker color. It will reach a length of about one inch.

This species is known from the Hawaiian Islands southward through Polynesia and across the tropical Pacific Ocean to the East Indies.

OSTERGAARD'S MITER SHELL   *Mitra ostergaardi* Pilsbry

Ostergaard's miter shell is a rather slender, spindle-shaped species which is marked by a series of six punctured lines upon the body whorl. The shell is dark brownish in color and is encircled by a light line at the shoulder. It will reach a length of more than one and one-half inches.

This species is known from the Hawaiian Islands. It was named for Mr. Jens M. Ostergaard of Honolulu.

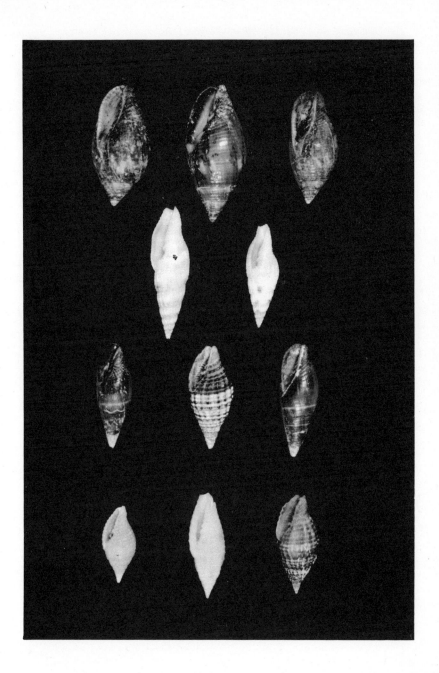

MISCELLANEOUS MITER SHELLS *Mitra* species

The shells figured in these rows are all species of puzzling and uncertain identity. They are all of small size and are from the Hawaiian Islands.

Lower Row, Right

THE PATRIARCHAL MITER SHELL *Pusia patriarchalis* (Gmelin)

The patriarchal miter shell is a small species with a turreted spire. The posterior part of the body whorl is marked by longitudinal ridges and furrows bearing nodules. It is marked at the anterior end by revolving ridges bearing small beady tubercles. The columella bears four plaits of which the posterior one is the largest. The shell is white at the posterior end, brownish at the middle of the body whorl, and bears a light colored band at the anterior end. It will reach three-fourths of an inch in length.

This species is distributed from the Hawaiian Islands southward and westward across the entire tropical Pacific Ocean to the Philippine Islands.

PEASE'S MITER SHELL   *Mitra peasei* Dohrn

Pease's miter shell is a slender, spindle-shaped species with a turreted, pointed spire, and deep sutures. It is marked over the outer surface by many revolving ribs and by fine longitudinal lines. The columella bears five plaits. It is whitish in color and is marked with orange brown upon the ridges. It is reported to reach a length of over three inches.

This species is known from the Hawaiian Islands and probably elsewhere in the Pacific area.

Some individuals regard this species as identical to *Mitra isabella* Swainson, a species from the western Pacific.

Upper Row, Center

MITER SHELL   *Mitra* species

This is a rare slender fusiform species of uncertain identity. It bears a pointed spire with slightly constricted sutures. The body whorl is encircled by about eleven large rows of rectangular tubercles while the other whorls bear but four or five rows. Between the rows of large tubercles are usually two smaller rows of like design. It will reach a length of at least one and one-fourth inches.

The specimen figured is from the Hawaiian Islands.

Second Row

THAANUM'S MITER SHELL   *Vexillum thaanumi* Pilsbry

Thaanum's miter shell is a slender spindle-shaped species marked by longitudinal ribs and interrupted spiral lines. It is colored with reddish and brownish markings. It will reach a length of one inch.

This species is known from the Hawaiian Islands and is named for Mr. Ditlev Thaanum of Honolulu.

Third Row, Left and Right

EMERSON'S MITER SHELL   *Mitra emersoni* Pilsbry

Emerson's miter shell is a slender, spindle-shaped species which is marked over its surface by both longitudinal and encircling lines. The columella bears four plaits. It is of a yellowish orange color marked by brown spots, lines, areas, and bands. It will exceed one inch in length.

This species, known first from the Hawaiian Islands, was named for Mr. Joseph Emerson of Honolulu.

Third Row, Center

CUMING'S MITER SHELL   *Pusia cumingi* (Reeve)

Cuming's miter shell is stout and spindle-shaped and bears a turreted spire. It has a rough exterior which is formed by longitudinal ribs crossed by smaller, rounded, revolving ribs. It may be either entirely white in color or white marked with brown. It will reach one and one-half inches in length.

This species extends from the Hawaiian Islands southward throughout Polynesia, across the Pacific Ocean to the Philippine Islands, through the East Indies, and across the Indian Ocean.

The Crenulated Miter Shell   *Pterygia crenulata* (Gmelin)

This shell is somewhat cylindrical in shape and bears a conical spire. It is distinguished by pitted encircling grooves, a long aperture, a thickened outer lip, and a smooth interior. It is white and is marked with clouded areas of brown often in the form of encircling bands. It will reach a length of one and one-half inches.

This species is distributed from the Hawaiian Islands southward throughout Polynesia, westward across the tropical Pacific Ocean to the Philippine Islands, through the East Indies, and across the Indian Ocean to the Red Sea.

The Lined Miter Shell   *Mitra paucilineata* (Dall)

This miter shell is a slender, somewhat spindle shaped species with a conical spire, an elongated aperture, a thick outer lip, and a smooth exterior marked by a few fine encircling lines. It is whitish in color and is covered in life with a brown epidermis. It reaches one inch in length.

This species is known from the Hawaiian Islands.

The Modest Miter Shell   *Mitra pudica* Pease

This miter shell is oval in outline and of short, stout construction. It is marked over the outer surface by many encircling ridges. It is white in color within and without. It exceeds one-half inch in length.

This species is known from the Hawaiian Islands.

THE HARP SHELL FAMILY

FAMILY HARPIDAE

The harp shells are a small but beautiful group of molluscs. They are nearly all shells of fairly large size and are longitudinally ribbed over the outer surface. The body whorl is large and broad and opens through a large aperture. This aperture is bordered on the outside by a lip which is thickened at its margin and on the inside by a broad and highly polished columella. There is no operculum.

The family is found in the tropical waters of the Pacific and Indian Oceans. Less than a dozen species are known.

Upper and Lower Rows

THE CONOIDAL HARP SHELL   *Harpa conoidalis* Lamarck

This harp shell is one of the most beautiful shells in the ocean. Like the other members of its family, it is a large species with a large flaring aperture and is decorated over the upper surface of the shell with heavy longitudinal ridges. The shell is white, brown, and black in color. There is a very large and conspicuous black spot upon the columella, the ribs upon the shell are crossed by dark lines, and the areas between the ribs are marked by a pattern of zig-zag lines. This harp shell ranges from two to four inches in length.

This mollusc is found from the Hawaiian Islands southward and westward through the warm waters of the tropical Pacific Ocean to the Philippine Islands, through the East Indies, and across the Indian Ocean to Mauritius and the coast of Africa.

Center

THE LITTLE LOVE HARP SHELL   *Harpa amouretta* Röding

This little harp shell is smaller and more elongated than *Harpa conoidalis* and its ribs are narrower and more widely separated. It is gray, chocolate, and white in color with pairs of short dark lines upon the ribs and with a zig-zag pattern between them. It ranges in length from three-fourths to one and one-half inches.

This is an Indo-Pacific species inhabiting the warm waters of the south seas.

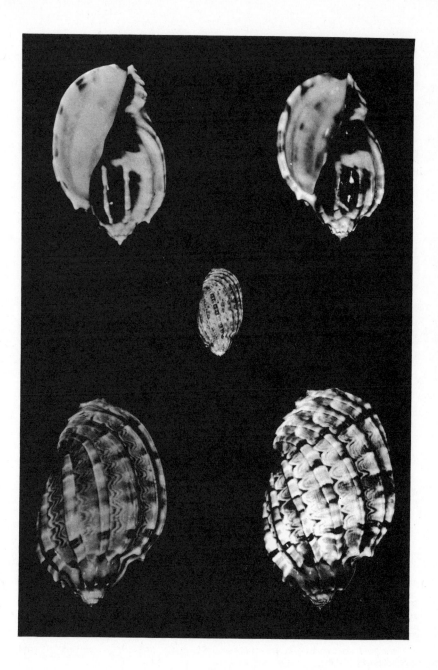

THE TURRET OR SLIT SHELL FAMILY
FAMILY TRURRIDAE (PLEUROTOMIDAE)

The family of the turret or slit shells is believed to be the largest family of molluscs living in the ocean for they are reported to include several thousand species. In general, these shells are spindle shaped, bear a turreted and pointed spire, and usually have a characteristic notch or slit in the outer lip near the suture. The columella is of varying length and usually ends in a straight canal. The group exhibits a wide variety of patterns and color markings and includes many species which are very beautiful. They vary in size from small and minute forms to species which are several inches in length. The family lives in both temperate and tropical seas. Specimens are usually obtained by dredging in the sand in the coastal waters bordering tropical and semi-tropical islands.

This group is often found in books under the name of *Pleurotoma*.

Upper Row
THE HORN SHAPED TURRET SHELL   *Turris* species

This turret shell is a beautiful species with a slender pointed spire. It is spirally ribbed with ridges of varying height and width. The interior of the aperture is white and smooth. The outer surface of the shell is a whitish cream color and is marked with dark oblong spots. It will reach a length of one and one-fourth inches.

This species is from the Hawaiian Islands. It is found in some collections under the name of *Turris cerithiformis*.

Middle Row, Left
TURRET SHELL   *Turris* species

This turret shell is probably an unnamed species. It bears an elongated anterior canal and is spirally grooved. The center of each whorl is marked by a wide raised band bearing somewhat rectangular tubercles which alternate with brown spots. It is cream and brownish in color. It will measure at least one and one-half inches in length. This species is from the Hawaiian Islands.

Middle Row, Right
THE LITTLE CHESTNUT TURRET SHELL   *Turris* species

This turret shell is spirally marked with ribs of varying height and width. The aperture is smooth within. It is dark yellowish brown in color and becomes progressively darker toward the anterior end. Large specimens seem to be darker in color than younger ones. It varies from one to two and one-half inches in length.

This species is found in the Hawaiian Islands and appears in some collections under the name of *Turris castanella*.

Lower Row
TURRET SHELL   *Turris* species

This turret shell is a slender species with a long tapering spire and a long anterior canal which is slightly curved. It is spirally grooved within the aperture and is marked externally by spiral ridges and by a wide raised encircling band bearing rectangular areas upon it. The color varies tremendously. It ranges from a pale yellow-brown to a dark brown on the outer surface and the anterior canal varies from white to brown within. The raised rectangular areas are always lighter than the rest of the shell.

This is a Hawaiian Islands species which is found in some collections under the name of *Turris aelomitra*.

164

THE CONE SHELL FAMILY

FAMILY CONIDAE

The cone shells are probably, next to the cowries, the most beautiful group of gastropod molluscs in the sea, for they exhibit a wide variety of colors to attract the collector's eye.

The shells of these molluscs are all conical in shape and have the narrower end of the cone directed toward the front of the animal. This inverse conical shape, in which the body whorls taper toward the front, is in marked contrast to most other shells of similar design.

The spire of these shells is usually low in height and the shells themselves are usually heavy and porcellanous in their makeup. The aperture is long and narrow extending nearly the full length of the shell and terminates in a notch at the small anterior end or base as it is sometimes called.

Some species of this family have a poison gland which discharges its poison to a slender dart with which the mollusc stings and benumbs its prey. Because of the ability of these shells to inflict severe wounds, shell collectors are very careful never to pick up cone shells by the small end.

This family includes more than five hundred species most of which make their home in the warm waters of the tropics.

THE OAK CONE *Conus quercinus* Hwass

The oak cone has a strong and heavy shell with a small, pointed spire. It is lemon yellow in color and is marked with many fine, close-set lines. It varies considerably in size but will reach a length of at least five inches.

This species is distributed from the Hawaiian Islands southward through Polynesia, across the entire tropical Pacific Ocean, through the East Indies, and across the Indian Ocean to the Red Sea.

This species occurs in most books under the name of *Conus cingulum* Martyn.

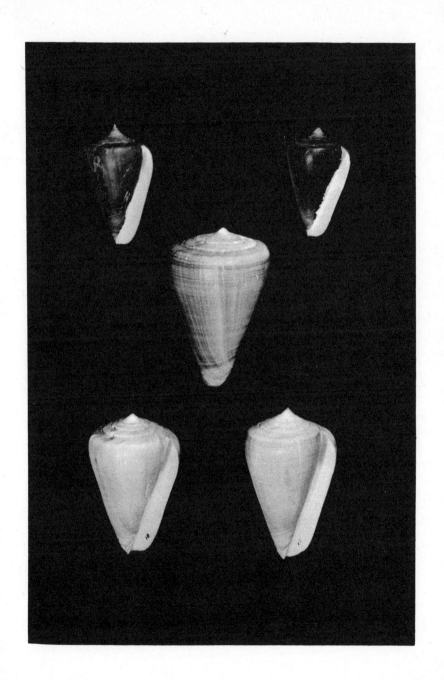

THE MARBLED CONE   *Conus marmoreus* Linnaeus

The marbled cone is a solid, heavy shell and has a low spire which is grooved and covered by tubercles. There are several color varieties of this species, but the shell is usually dark brown or chocolate in color and is marked by slightly rounded, white or pinkish, triangular spots. It will reach approximately five inches in length.

This species inhabits the warm waters of the globe from the Hawaiian Islands southward and westward through all of the islands of the tropical Pacific and Indian Oceans.

The marbled cone is one of several species of cone shells which is capable of inflicting a very severe wound with its poison dart and should therefore be handled only by the large end when it is alive.

The species figured above is often found in collections under the name of *Conus marmoreus* Linnaeus variety *bandanus* Hwass. It is the variety in which the white triangular markings are crowded so as to give the appearance of two encircling irregular bands.

THE LEOPARD CONE   *Conus leopardus* Röding

This cone shell is one of the largest and heaviest members of its family. It is a heavy, ponderous species of a rather uniform conical shape and is characterized by a low spire with a groove upon the top or shoulder of each whorl. It is generally white in color both within and without and is marked over the surface with spiral rows of dark spots.

This species is distributed from the Hawaiian Islands southward and westward throughout Polynesia, the islands of the south seas, through the East Indies, and across the Indian Ocean.

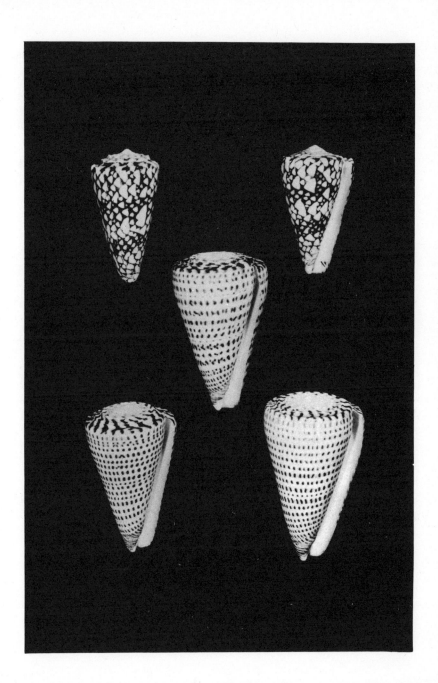

THE IMPERIAL CONE   *Conus imperialis* Linnaeus

The imperial cone is a slender, handsome species and has a low spire which is covered by tubercles. It is yellowish or whitish in color, encircled by two wide brown bands, and marked by many spots and bars which are arranged in transverse rows. It will reach three or more inches in length.

This is an Indo-Pacific species and occurs from the Hawaiian Islands southward and westward through Polynesia, the islands of the south Pacific, the East Indies, and across the Indian Ocean to the coast of Africa.

THE STRIATED CONE   *Conus striatus* Linnaeus

The striated cone is a large and heavy shell, slightly constricted at the shoulder or posterior end, and marked by a great many fine revolving lines. The spire has a spiral groove which follows the whorls of the shell. The entire shell is whitish in color, stained with pale rose red, and variously spotted and streaked with black. This shell will reach five inches in length and like *Conus marmoreus* possesses a poisonous sting.

This species is found from the Hawaiian Islands southward and westward throughout Polynesia, across the tropical Pacific Ocean, through the East Indies, and across the Indian Ocean to the Red Sea.

THE DISTANTLY LINED CONE   *Conus distans* Bruguiere

This large cone is marked with tubercles upon the spire and is usually somewhat constricted near the middle of the shell. It is nearly always encircled by distant or widely spaced impressed lines. It is variously colored with yellow and brown on the outside and is usually white or violet tinted within. This species will reach five inches in length.

This cone is distributed from the Hawaiian Islands southward through Polynesia to New Zealand and westward through the islands of the tropical Pacific Ocean to the Philippine Islands and the East Indies.

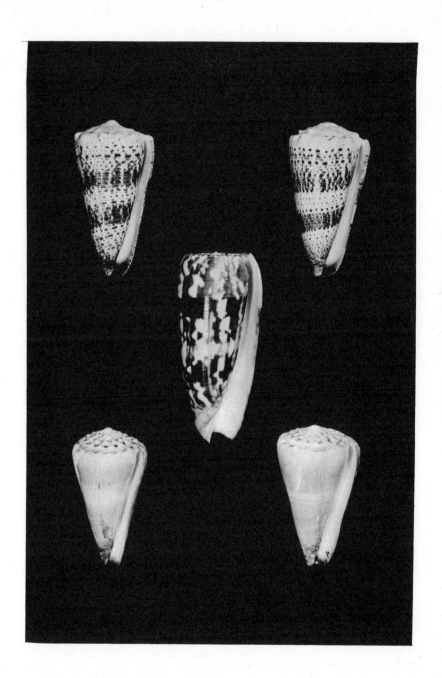

THE HEBREW CONE   *Conus ebraeus* Linnaeus

The Hebrew cone is a fairly heavy and solid shell. It is whitish in color without and is marked by three or four dark bands composed of somewhat rhomboidal spots. Within the aperture the shell is whitish in color with faintly clouded areas corresponding to the external pattern on the shell. It will reach a length of about one and three-fourths inches.

This species is found from the Hawaiian Islands southward and westward through Polynesia, the islands of the south Pacific, the East Indies, and across the Indian Ocean to the coast of Africa.

Upper Row, Center

THE NUSSATELLA CONE   *Conus nussatella* Linnaeus

This cone shell is a slender species of light weight and with a fairly well developed spire. It is whitish in color without, blotched with orange-brown, and encircled by minutely granular ridges and small dark brown spots. It will reach a length of about two and one-half inches.

This mollusc is distributed from the Hawaiian Islands southward and westward throughout Polynesia and the islands of the south seas, through the East Indies, and across the Indian Ocean to Africa and the Red Sea.

Middle Row

THE CAT CONE   *Conus catus* Bruguiere

The shell of the cat cone is quite stout and heavy and is marked in a characteristic manner with spiral nodulose ridges at the anterior or basal end of the body whorl. Externally the shell is colored with various shades of brown and irregularly marked with white. It will reach a length of one and one-fourth inches.

This species is distributed from the Hawaiian Islands southward through Polynesia, westward through the island of the south seas, through the East Indies, and across the Indian Ocean to Africa and the Red Sea.

Lower Row, Right and Left

THE SOLDIER CONE   *Conus miles* Linnaeus

The soldier cone is of medium size and is marked by spiral ridges at the anterior or basal end. It is of a yellowish white color and is marked by many wavy, longitudinal, threadlike, brownish lines and by a chocolate band about the middle of the shell; the anterior end is also dark in color. It will reach a length of about two and seven-eighths inches.

This species is found from the Hawaiian Islands southward and westward throughout Polynesia and the islands of the south Pacific, through the East Indies, the Philippine Islands and southern Japan, and across the Indian Ocean to the coast of Africa.

Lower Row, Center

THE RETIFORM CONE   *Conus retifer* Menke

The retiform cone is somewhat pear-shaped, has a well developed spire, and bears fine, raised, revolving lines at the anterior or basal end. It is orange-brown in color and is marked by longitudinal brown bands and by triangular white areas which are grouped in a band near the anterior, the middle, and the posterior end of the shell. It will reach a length of about two and one-half inches.

This species is found from the Hawaiian Islands southward and westward through the tropical Pacific to the Philippines and the East Indies.

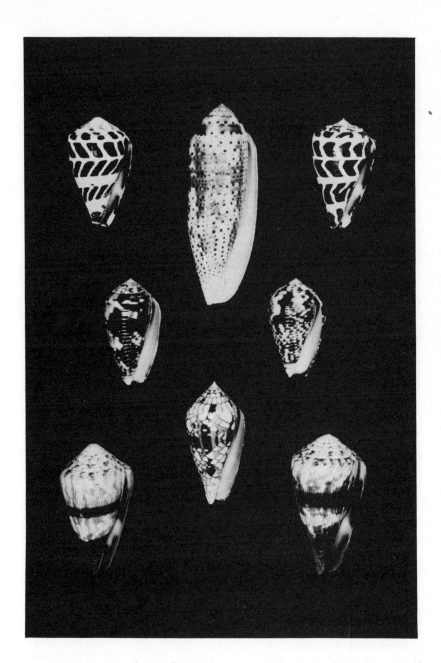

THE PENNIFORM CONE   *Conus pennaceus* Born

This cone shell is fairly heavy and robust in construction and quite wide at the shoulder; the spire is of medium height and is concave in outline. The color of this species varies somewhat, but it is usually of an orange-brown color and covered with small white dots and with larger white tri-angular spots which often form a band at the shoulder or near the middle of the shell. It will reach a length of about two and one-half inches.

This species is distributed from the Hawaiian Islands southward and westward through Polynesia, the islands of the south Pacific, through the East Indies, and across the Indian Ocean to Africa and the Red Sea.

Upper Center

THE WOVEN CONE   *Conus textile* Linnaeus

The woven cone is a large species of medium weight with a wide, white aperture bordered by a curving lip and with a well developed spire which is straight in outline. It is yellowish brown in color, is marked with wavy, longitudinal lines, and is covered with small, white, triangular spots which seem to group themselves into three poorly defined bands which are placed at the anterior end, at the center, and at the shoulder of the shell. It will reach a length of about five inches.

This species is distributed from the Hawaiian Islands southward and westward through Polynesia, the islands of the south Pacific, through the East Indies, and across the Indian Ocean to Africa and the Red Sea.

Middle Row, Right and Left

THE SUMATRA CONE   *Conus sumatrensis* Lamarck

The shell of this species is quite heavy and sturdy in its construction. It is light yellow in color and marked with irregular, longitudinal, brownish lines which are often interrupted near the center to form an irregular whit-ish band about the middle of the body whorl. It will reach a length of five inches.

This species is distributed from the Hawaiian Islands southward and westward through all of the islands of the tropical Pacific and Indian Oceans to the Red Sea and the coast of Africa.

Lower Center

THE CALF CONE   *Conus vitulinus* Bruguiere

The calf cone is a fairly heavy species with a low spire. It is marked at the anterior end of the body whorl by small spiral, granular ridges. This shell is orange-brown to chocolate in color and is marked at the posterior end and again near the middle of the shell with white bands which are crossed by wavy, longitudinal brown lines. It will reach a length of about three inches. This species is distributed from the Hawaiian Islands southward through Polynesia and westward through the islands of the south Pacific, through the East Indies, and across the Indian Ocean.

Lower Row, Right and Left

THE FLEA CONE   *Conus pulicarius* Bruguiere

The flea cone is quite heavy and solid in construction and is marked with tubercles on the spire. It is whitish in color and is covered with dark spots which are usually more numerous at the anterior end. It will reach a length of about two and three-fourths inches.

This species is distributed from the Hawaiian Islands southward through Polynesia, and then westward through the islands of the tropical Pacific to southern Japan and throughout the East Indies.

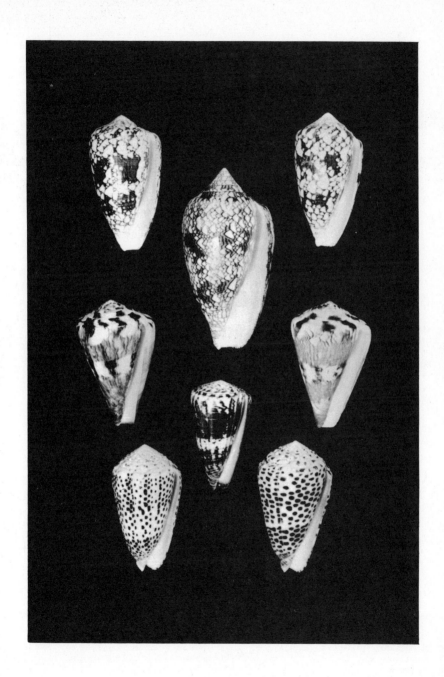

Upper Row

THE RAT CONE   *Conus rattus* Bruguiere

The rat cone is of medium size and of quite heavy construction. It is yellowish brown in color and marked by large white spots about the shoulder and by an interrupted band of white spots about the center of the shell. It will reach a length of about two inches.

The rat cone is distributed from the Hawaiian Islands southward throughout Polynesia, westward through the islands of the tropical Pacific to the East Indies, and across the Indian Ocean to Africa and the Red Sea.

Second Row

CONE SHELL   *Conus hammatus* Bartsch and Rehder

This cone is an average sized species without many significant characters. The spire is quite elevated and spirally grooved and the shoulder of the body whorl shows a very slight tendency toward knobs. The aperture is narrow and the outer lip is thin and sharp. It is buff in color and variously banded; it is marked upon the spire with reddish brown. The interior of the aperture is bluish white. It resembles *Conus lividus* somewhat but lacks the purple tip at the anterior end. It will reach a length of about one and three-fourths inches.

This species is known only from dredgings about Hawaii.

Third Row

THE BLUISH CONE   *Conus lividus* Bruguiere

The bluish cone may be recognized by the fact that its spire is covered by tubercles and also that the body whorl is marked at the anterior end by fine spiral ridges with granules upon them. The shell is usually white in color upon the spire, orange-brown on the body whorl, and rose colored at the anterior end of the shell. The interior of the aperture is violet colored. It will reach a length of two and one-half inches.

This species is distributed from the Hawaiian Islands southward throughout Polynesia and westward through the islands of the tropical Pacific, through the East Indies, and across the Indian Ocean to the Red Sea.

Fourth Row, Right and Left

THE GOLDEN YELLOW CONE   *Conus flavidus* Lamarck

The golden yellow cone is a moderately slender species with a fairly firm and heavy shell. It is yellowish brown on the outside and is marked about the middle and at the posterior part of the body whorl by a white band which is often difficult to distinguish. The anterior end of the shell is tipped with purple; the aperture within is also marked with purple and shows the external white band. It will reach a length of over two inches.

This species extends from the Hawaiian Islands southward and westward through the islands of Polynesia and the south Pacific Ocean, through the East Indies, and across the Indian Ocean to the Red Sea.

Lower Row, Center

SPICER'S CONE   *Conus spiceri* Bartsch

This cone shell is described on page 178. The specimen figured here shows the periostracum upon the shell.

Upper Row, Right and Left

THE MORELET'S CONE   *Conus moreleti* Crosse

The indistinct cone is a slender, narrow species resembling *Conus lividus* Brug. The spire is low and covered with tubercles and the body whorl is marked with striae at its anterior or small end. The shell is a yellowish brown color and marked with white upon the tubercles, a faint white area about the shoulder, and with a very faint white band about the lower middle of the shell. It is violet at the anterior end and in the aperture. It will reach a length of about two inches.

This species is found from Hawaii to the Philippine Islands.

SPICER'S CONE   *Upper Center*   *Conus spiceri* Bartsch

Spicer's cone is of moderate size, quite slender in shape, and very regular in outline. It is of a pale yellow color on the exterior surface and is bluish white within the aperture. The exterior of the shell is covered by an umber colored periostracum. It is about two and one-half inches in length. It is named for Mr. V. D. P. Spicer of Centralia, Washington.

The shell is at present known only from the Hawaiian Islands.

Center Row

THE ERMINE CONE   *Conus ermineus* Born

This cone shell has a low, unornamented spire and is marked by a few striae upon the body whorl which become a little granular toward the anterior end. It is a dark brownish color and is marked by a variable row of white spots or by a white band at the shoulder of the whorl; it also bears a row of spots or a band of varying size and intensity just anterior to the middle of the body. The anterior or base of the shell is darker than the rest. It will reach a length of two inches.

This species is distributed from the Hawaiian Islands southward through the islands of Melanesia, westward through the tropical Pacific to the Philippine Islands, through the East Indies, and across the Indian Ocean at least as far as Ceylon.

The correct name for this species is believed to be *Conus inermis* Born.

Lower Center

THE PRICKED OR PERFORATED CONE   *Conus pertusus* Bruguiere

The surface of this shell is covered by fine striae which bear minute punctures. The spire is slightly convex in outline and very slightly turreted. It is rose and yellow in color and is marked with white areas at the shoulder and at the middle of the body whorl; these white areas may be spaced to form an interrupted band or run somewhat together to form a more solid band. It will reach two inches in length.

This species is distributed from the Hawaiian Islands southward and westward through the tropical Pacific Ocean to the Philippine Islands, through the East Indies, and across the Indian Ocean to Madagascar.

Lower Row, Right and Left

THE ABBREVIATED CONE   *Conus miliaris* Hwass variety *abbreviatus* Reeve

This cone shell is short and broad, has a depressed spire, and is encircled by striae bearing quite regularly spaced tubercles. It is a bluish gray color marked by paler bands encircling the shell and by spiral rows of dark brown spots. It will reach a length of one and one-fourth inches.

Conus miliaris Hwass is a widely distributed species. It is found from the Galapagos Islands and the Hawaiian Islands southward and westward through Polynesia, Micronesia, Melanesia, through the East Indies, and across the Indian Ocean to the Red Sea and the coast of Africa. The variety known as *abbreviatus* is known only from the Hawaiian Islands. Some individuals regard this variety as a separate species.

178

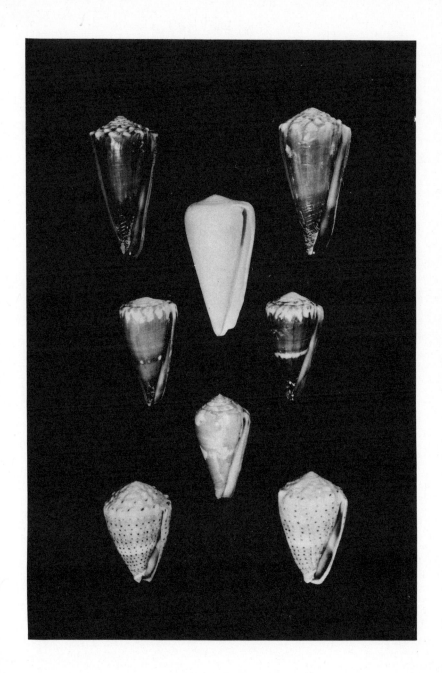

THE DUSKY OR OBSCURE CONE   *Conus obscurus* Reeve

This cone is of medium size, oval in outline, and light in weight. The spire is quite well developed and the suture of the last whorl descends well below the spire. The outer lip is thin, flaring in outline, and encloses an aperture which is wide, particularly at the anterior end. The shell is yellowish brown in color and is marked by irregular flesh colored areas. It will reach a length of about one and one-fourth inches. It is known only from the Hawaiian Islands.

This shell is also known as *Conus halitropus* Bartsch and Rehder.

THE CYLINDRICAL CONE   *Conus cylindraceus* Broderip and Sowerby

The cylindrical cone is spindle shaped and is marked over the outer surface by many fine revolving striae and by small granules toward the anterior end. The spire is well developed and pointed. The shell is yellowish brown or chestnut colored and is marked by wavy longitudinal bands of white which may be expanded to form an anterior and posterior band of white about the shell. It will reach a length of one and one-half inches.

This species is known from the Hawaiian Islands southward and westward through the islands of central Polynesia and Melanesia.

THE NAIL CONE OR CLUB CONE   *Conus clavus* Linnaeus

This cone shell is cylindrical in form, light in weight and its aperture, which is bordered by a thin lip, becomes wider anteriorly. The spire is well developed and the outer surface is marked by revolving striae. The shell is orange brown in color and is covered with a network of small lines which enclose light colored triangular areas of varying size. There is a tendency for the shell to be marked by two brownish horizontal bands. It will reach a length of about two inches.

This species is distributed from the Hawaiian Islands southward and westward throughout Polynesia and across the warm tropical waters of the Pacific Ocean to Japan and the Philippine Islands.

This species somewhat resembles *Conus textile* in its color pattern. A variety of this species known as *Conus clavus* Linnaeus variety *dactylosus* Kiener has a reticulated color pattern of a more uniform size and exhibits quite well developed bands about the shell.

THE TRUE LINED CONE   *Conus eugrammatus* Bartsch and Rehder

This mollusc bears a small, cone-shaped shell with a prominent spire and a well developed apex. The spire is marked with an encircling row of nodules and the body whorl with spiral grooves. In life the shell is covered by a thin, light gray periostracum. The shell is pale bluff in color and is clouded and spotted with brownish areas; the outer lip is yellowish white within. It will reach a length of about one inch.

This species is at present known only from shallow water dredgings about the Hawaiian Islands.

THE CEYLON CONE   *Conus ceylanensis nanus* Sowerby

The Ceylon cone is a small species varying widely in its form and color. The shoulder of the body whorl is marked by low tubercles and the anterior half of the shell is marked by revolving rows of small tubercles. The shell is white in color and variously marked with chestnut usually in the pattern of a row of small dots between the tubercles that ornament the shoulder of the body whorl and also forming a band of interrupted zig-zag lines about the middle of the shell. The anterior tip of the shell is marked with violet. The shell will reach a length of about one and one-fourth inches although most individuals are much smaller.

This species is known from the Hawaiian Islands southward through Polynesia, and then westward through the islands of the south seas, through the East Indies, and across the Indian Ocean to the Red Sea and the coast of Africa.

THE BUBBLE CONE   *Conus bullatus* Linnaeus

The bubble cone is thin, light in weight, and more bulbous than most members of its group. It has a fairly prominent spire and apex, a thin curved outer lip, and an aperture which becomes wider anteriorly. The body whorl is marked by grooves toward the anterior end. The shell is whitish in color marked with orange, reddish, and brownish in a fine irregular manner and forming indistinct bands about the body whorl; the aperture is pinkish within. It will reach a length of about three inches.

This mollusc extends from the Hawaiian Islands southward and westward through the warm tropical water of the Pacific Ocean to the Philippine Islands.

THE CHALDEAN CONE   *Conus chaldaeus* (Röding)

The worm cone resembles the Hebrew cone, *Conus ebraeus* Linnaeus, and is regarded by some individuals as a variety of that species. It is however smaller in size, has a rougher exterior, and has the white markings in the form of interrupted zig-zag lines. It will reach a maximum length of one and one-half inches.

This mollusc is distributed from the Hawaiian Islands southward and westward through the islands of the south Pacific Ocean, through the East Indies, and across the Indian Ocean.

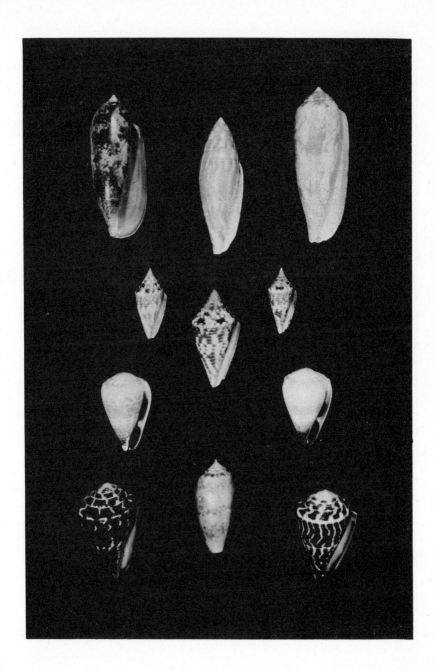

THE AUGER SHELL FAMILY

FAMILY TEREBRIDAE

The auger shells are very slender, elongated sea shells, many of which have beautiful colors and color patterns. They are constructed of many flat-sided whorls which taper very gradually and evenly toward the pointed apex. The aperture of these shells contains a small notch in front, the columella is without plaits, and the operculum is of a horny texture.

The group is found in warm waters of the temperate and tropical seas where they burrow in the sand. The family is a large one containing about two hundred species.

THE CRENULATED AUGER SHELL — *Terebra crenulata* (Linnaeus)

This auger shell is marked by a turret at the sutures and by nodules scattered in a row around the posterior part of the body whorl just anterior to the suture. The shell is of a fleshy cream color and is decorated by rows of spots and wavy lines about the sutures. It will reach about five inches in length.

This species extends from the Hawaiian Islands southward throughout Polynesia and across the entire Pacific and Indian Oceans.

A variety of this species known as *Terebra crenulata* (Linnaeus) variety *interlineata* Deshayes differs from the typical species in having a smoother shell and in lacking the spiral row of coronations or knobs about the sutures.

Left

THE AWL-SHAPED OR SUBULATE AUGER SHELL   *Terebra subulata* (Linn.)

This auger shell is of an unusually slender shape and has a very smooth surface. It is of a yellowish flesh color and is marked with somewhat rectangular brownish spots. It will reach six inches in length.

This species is distributed from the Hawaiian Islands southward throughout Polynesia and westward across the Pacific Ocean to Japan and the Philippine Islands, through the East Indies, and across the Indian Ocean to the Red Sea.

Center

THE SPOTTED AUGER SHELL   *Terebra maculata* (Linnaeus)

This mollusc has a thick, heavy shell composed of smooth shining whorls. It is of a flesh color with a nearly white interior and is marked externally by a varied pattern of black or purplish black areas. It is the largest species in the family and may measure over eight inches in length.

This species extends from the Hawaiian Islands southward throughout Polynesia, along the coast of Australia, and westward through the Philippine Islands and the East Indies.

Right

THE WHITE SPOTTED SHELL   *Terebra guttata* (Röding)

This auger shell is a slender species of medium weight with sutures which are somewhat constricted. It is orange-brown in color and is marked with two rows of white spots upon the body whorl and by one row upon the earlier whorls. It will reach five inches in length.

This species extends from the Hawaiian Islands southward and westward throughout the tropical Pacific Ocean and through the islands of the East Indies.

THE DARK SPOTTED AUGER SHELL   *Terebra aureolata* (L1,k)

This auger shell is a beautiful, long, tapering species in which each whorl is marked by three rows of dark chocolate spots. It varies in length from three to six inches.

This species is distributed from the Hawaiian Islands southward throughout Polynesia and then westward across the tropical Pacific Ocean to Japan and the Philippine Islands.

THE ARGUS AUGER SHELL   *Terebra argus* Hinds

The argus auger shell is a rather slender species with a fairly smooth surface, particularly at the anterior end. The shell is marked at the posterior end by longitudinal plications and by an encircling groove placed anterior to the sutures; both of these markings become less pronounced and tend to disappear toward the anterior end. The shell is white in color and is usually marked by very light, somewhat rectangular, yellowish brown spots which form four spiral rows upon the body whorl and two upon the rest of the shell. It will reach a length of about five inches.

This species is distributed from the Hawaiian Islands southward throughout Polynesia and possibly elsewhere in the Indo-Pacific area.

A variety of this species, in which the shell is shorter and the whorls less oblique, has been described and named *Terebra argus* Hinds variety *brachygyra* Pilsbry.

THE DIVIDED AUGER SHELL   *Terebra dimidiata* (Linnaeus)

This slender auger shell is marked by a spiral groove at the posterior side of each whorl and by longitudinal ribs upon those whorls which are nearest to the apex of the spire. It is reddish orange in color and is marked by streaks and bands of white. It will reach a length of about five inches.

This species is distributed from the Hawaiian Islands southward throughout Polynesia and westward across the tropical Pacific Ocean to the East Indies.

AUGER SHELL   *Terebra* species

This auger shell is a medium sized species, rather stout in outline, and of rather heavy construction. The entire surface is smooth and is marked by an encircling spiral groove just anterior to the suture; this groove becomes less pronounced toward the anterior end. It is whitish or yellowish in color and measures about two inches in length.

This species is found in the Hawaiian Islands and possibly elsewhere in the Pacific area. It is of puzzling identity and appears in various collections under the name of *Terebra candida* (Born).

THE YELLOW AUGER SHELL   *Terebra chlorata* Lamarck

This species is encircled by a faint groove anterior to the suture. It is a smooth shell anteriorly, but becomes increasingly crenate toward the apex. It is white, yellow, or green in color and is marked with longitudinal brownish streaks and splashes. It will reach four inches in length.

This auger shell is distributed from the Hawaiian Islands southward and westward across the entire tropical Pacific Ocean, through the islands of the East Indies, and across the Indian Ocean to the coast of Africa.

THE WHITE SPOTTED SHELL   *Terebra guttata* (Röding)

The eyed auger shell is a slender species in which the whorls are somewhat constricted at their middle and show a tendency toward turreting. The shell is orange-brown in color and is marked by a row of large white spots just anterior to the suture and by two rows of large white spots upon the body whorl. It will reach a length of five inches.

This species is distributed from the Hawaiian Islands southward and described and named *Terebra lanceata* (Linnaeus) variety *oahuensis* Pilsbry.

THE LANCED AUGER SHELL   *Terebra lanceata* (Linnaeus)

The lanced auger shell is a smooth and shining species in which the whorls are somewhat truncated and slightly swollen anterior to the sutures. It is of a glistening white color and is marked by wavy, longitudinal, oblique, brown lines. It measures about two inches in length.

This species is distributed from the Hawaiian Islands southward through Polynesia and westward across the tropical Pacific Ocean, through the islands of the East Indies, and across the Indian Ocean to the coast of Africa.

A smaller form of this species from the island of Oahu has been described and named *Terebra lanceata* Linnaeus variety *oahuensis* Pilsbry.

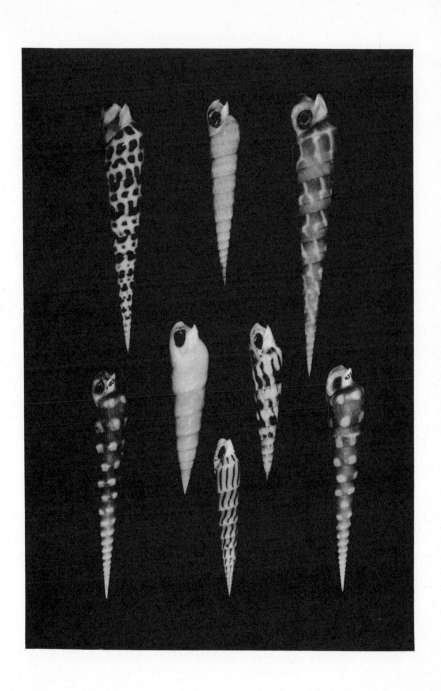

THE VARIABLE AUGER SHELL   *Terebra inconstans* Hinds

This species is covered over the outer surface of the shell by a pattern of longitudinal angular ridges or plications. It has a wide flaring aperture and lacks the encircling spiral groove anterior to the suture which is found on many of these shells. The color of this species is extremely variable but is usually of a chocolate, ash, or bluish color with a white band encircling the suture; it will vary in intensity from light to dark. It measures about one and one-half inches in length.

This auger shell is distributed from the Hawaiian Islands southward throughout Polynesia, across the entire tropical Pacific Ocean, and through the East Indies.

This is an extremely variable species which is somewhat difficult to identify. It is found in books under a variety of names.

Second Row, Right and Left

THE LEADEN AUGER SHELL   *Terebra plumbea* Quoy and Gaimard

The leaden auger shell is marked over its outer surface by many straight, smooth, longitudinal folds or plications. It is of a bluish lead-gray color or may be yellowish brown in color and is usually marked by light bands at the sutures. It will reach one inch in length.

This species is distributed from the Hawaiian Islands southward to Australia and westward through the tropical Pacific Ocean to the coast of Asia and the East Indies.

Third Row

THE SHINING AUGER SHELL   *Terebra nitida* Hinds

This mollusc is of small size and is marked over the outer surface by many longitudinal plications or folds. The outer surface of the shell is smooth and glistening and there is a row of punctures in the grooves just anterior to the sutures. The aperture is narrow. The shell is whitish or very light-tan in color and will reach a length in excess of one inch.

This species is distributed from the Hawaiian Islands southward through Polynesia and probably elsewhere in the Pacific area.

This species is also known by the name of *Terebra plicatella* Deshayes.

Lower Row

PEASE'S AUGER SHELL   *Terebra peasei* Deshayes

Pease's auger shell has a smooth exterior which is marked by longitudinal folds and by a spiral groove just anterior to the suture which forms a band about the shell on about the posterior one-third of each whorl. It varies considerably in color. It will range from white through various degrees of yellow and orange to chocolate and may bear a pattern of longitudinal brownish markings upon about every third or fourth fold. The sutural band is usually whitish in color.

This species is distributed from the Hawaiian Islands southward and westward through all of the warm tropical Pacific waters to the Philippine Islands and through the East Indies.

Some authorities regard this mollusc as a variety of the cancellated auger shell, *Terebra cancellata* Quoy and Gaimard.

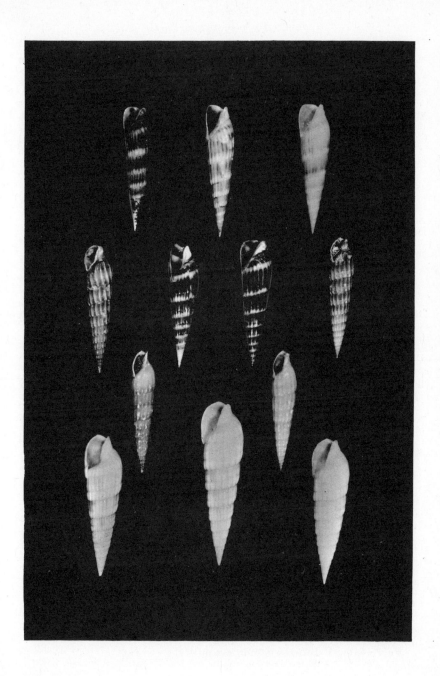

Upper Row, Right and Left

THAANUM'S AUGER SHELL   *Terebra thaanumi* Pilsbry

Thaanum's auger shell is one of the smaller Pacific species and is difficult to identify because it so closely resembles another species described as *Terebra gouldi* Deshayes. It is moderately slender, straight in outline, and is covered over the outer surface by many smooth, longitudinal ribs. It is encircled anterior to the suture by a groove which marks off a rather wide presutural band; this band is approximately one-third of the width of the whorl. It is a light colored shell of a pinkish buff tint upon which are vague, indistinct, and poorly defined reddish brown markings. It reaches two inches in length. This species occurs in Hawaiian waters.

Upper Row, Center Pair

GOULD'S AUGER SHELL   *Terebra gouldi* Deshayes

Gould's auger shell is a species of medium size in which each whorl is marked posteriorly by a spiral groove. The whorls are marked with close set longitudinal ribs on the anterior side of the groove and by low knobs posterior to the groove. It is of a yellowish white color with the body whorl marked by three spiral bands and the remaining whorls marked by two spiral chestnut bands. It reaches a length of about two and one-half inches. This species occurs in Hawaii and elsewhere in the tropical Pacific area. This mollusc closely resembles *Terebra thaanumi* Pilsbry.

Middle Row

THE PRICKED OR PUNCTURED AUGER SHELL   *Terebra pertusa* Born

The punctured auger shell is a slender species which is straight in outline. It is marked by fine longitudinal folds and by an encircling groove anterior to the sutures which divides the longitudinal folds into two parts upon each whorl. There is a longer, more slender, anterior part which is encircled by rows of punctures and a posterior part which has somewhat the appearance of a row of beads. The color of this shell varies considerably. It ranges from white through yellow, orange, purple and chocolate to black. This color is applied in clouded areas over the surface, often with dark spots upon the beady band bordering the sutures. It will reach a length of about three inches. This species is distributed from the Hawaiian Islands southward through the Pacific Ocean to Australia and elsewhere in the tropical Pacific area.

Lower Row, Right and Left

SPALDING'S AUGER SHELL   *Terebra spaldingi* Pilsbry

Spalding's auger shell is a fairly robust species in outline and is marked over the entire outer surface with smooth longitudinal ribs. It has an encircling groove anterior to the suture which marks off the presutural band. It is whitish in color and is marked with flesh colored tints in the grooves and about the sutural band. It measures about one and one-half inches in length. This species occurs in the Hawaiian Islands.

Lower Center

THE RELATED AUGER SHELL   *Terebra propinqua* Pease

This auger shell is a slender species in which the whorls are crossed by longitudinal plications and encircled by a groove just anterior to the suture. The shell is predominately brown in color and is marked with white blotches and streaks. Many of the short beady plications bordering the suture are marked with white. It measures about one and one-half inches. This species occurs in Hawaii and elsewhere in the Pacific area.

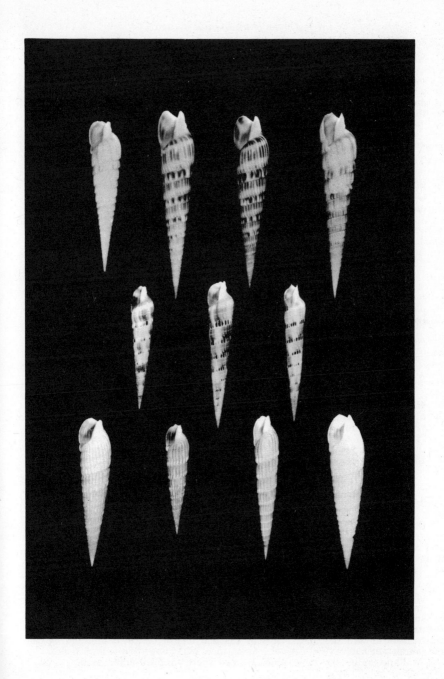

Upper Row, Right and Left

THE TIGER SPOTTED AUGER SHELL   *Terebra felina* (Dillwyn)

This mollusc has a fairly firm and heavy shell which is smooth on the exterior except for an encircling groove anterior to each suture. The shell varies in color from white to flesh color and is marked on each whorl by a single encircling row of brown spots posterior to each suture and by a double row of spots upon the body whorl. It will reach a length of about three inches.

This species is found from Hawaii southward throughout Polynesia.

Upper Row, Center Pair

THE CORDED AUGER SHELL..   *Terebra funiculata* Hinds

This auger shell is a slender, turreted, screw-shaped species marked by a small aperture and by large, revolving, rounded ribs, the largest of which is next to the suture. It is of a tan or brownish color and will reach a length of about two inches.

This species is found from Hawaii southward throughout Polynesia.

Middle Row, Right and Left

THE STRAW COLORED AUGER SHELL   *Terebra staminea* Gray

This slender, turreted species is encircled by two beady bands anterior to the suture of which the posterior band is by far the larger. The remainder of each whorl is crossed by fine revolving lines and by longitudinal growth lines. It is straw colored or orange with white sutural bands. It will reach a length of two and one-half inches.

This species is distributed from the Hawaiian Islands southward and westward across the tropical Pacific to the Philippines and the coast of Asia.

Middle Row, Center

THE BABYLONIAN AUGER SHELL   *Terebra babylonia* Lamarck

The Babylonian auger shell is often shown as a variety of *Terebra staminea* Gray which it closely resembles. It may not be a separate species although it seems to differ from *T. staminea* in being larger, longer, less turreted, lighter in color, and with the beady sutural band less prominent. It will reach a length of at least two and one-half inches.

This species is distributed from the Hawaiian Islands southward through Polynesia and thence across the tropical Pacific to the coast of Asia.

Lower Row, Right and Left

THE SHORT-WHORLED AUGER SHELL   *Terebra argus* Hinds v. *brachygyra* P.

This mollusc is a smaller variety of *Terebra argus* Hinds in which the shell is shorter, the whorls are less oblique, and the color pattern less distinct. It is from the Hawaiian Islands.

Lower Row, Center Pair

THE VERREAUX'S AUGER SHELL   *Hastula verreauxi* (Deshayes)

This auger shell is a beautiful, slender, polished species which is marked by longitudinal ridges which in some specimens become fainter anteriorly. The shell is light yellow in color and is marked by a white spiral band just anterior to the suture and also by a spiral series of very dark brown or purplish spots which become smaller, farther apart, and fainter toward the apex. It will reach a length of about one and three-fourths inches.

This mollusc is found from Hawaii southward throughout Polynesia.

THE PENCILLED AUGER SHELL   *Terebra penicillata* Hinds

The pencilled auger shell is a beautiful smooth species which is marked by a variable pattern of longitudinal wavy brown lines which are wider behind the sutures and which may even touch or merge with adjoining lines to form an irregular band around the upper or middle part of the whorl. It will reach a length of about two inches.

This species is distributed from the Hawaiian Islands southward and westward across the entire tropical Pacific and Indian Oceans.

THE NODULAR AUGER SHELL   *Terebra nodularis* Deshayes

This auger shell is one of the smaller species of confusing and uncertain identity; it is regarded by some as a synonym of *Terebra textilis* Hinds. It is apparently a variable species, slender in outline, with straight sides, and marked upon the surface by two encircling bands of longitudinal striae. It is yellowish white to tan in color. It ranges from one to one and one-half inches in length.

This species is distributed from the Hawaiian Islands southward and westward to Japan and the islands of the East Indies.

THE CURVED AUGER SHELL   *Terebra inflexa* Pease variety *alta* Dall

This small species is covered over the outside by smooth, rounded, longitudinal ribs or plications. It is of a very light tan color and is marked with two darker encircling bands. It is about one inch in length. This variety is found in the Hawaiian Islands.

AUGER SHELL   *Terebra* species

This little auger shell is an undetermined species from the Hawaiian Islands. It is a slender, highly polished species and is marked longitudinally by angular ridges and angular grooves. A constriction encircles each whorl about one-fourth of the distance from the posterior end. It is dark brown to blackish in color and measures about one-half inch in length.

This species occurs in the Hawaiian Islands and possibly elsewhere in the Pacific area.

AUGER SHELL   *Terebra* species

This species is longitudinally grooved on the posterior half of each whorl and smooth on the anterior half. The end of the spire is rounded due to a large protoconch. The shell is pale yellow ir color and is marked anterior to each suture by a white area and by a spiral row of light brown spots. It will reach a length of about three-fourths of an inch.

The auger shell figured here is an undetermined species from the Hawaiian Islands and possibly elsewhere in the Pacific area.

THE WHITE AUGER SHELL   *Terebra albula* Menke

The white auger shell is a small species marked by longitudinal plications or folds which do not extend entirely across the whorls. These folds are best developed at the posterior side of the whorl and become less distinct and even disappear anteriorly. Toward the posterior side of each whorl these folds develop into small knobs so as to give the suture a knobby or coronated aspect. It is whitish in color and is banded with tan or orange-brown.

This mollusc is distributued from the Hawaiian Islands southward to Australia and westward across the tropical Pacific Ocean to the Philippine Islands and the East Indies.

Some individuals regard this species as a Pacific variety of the West Indian form known as *Terebra hastata* Gmelin.

AUGER SHELL   *Terebra* species

This little auger shell is an undetermined species somewhat resembling *Terebra plicatella* but differing in its color and in its more highly polished surface. It is marked by somewhat angular longitudinal ridges and by longitudinal grooves each of which bears a pit placed forward of the suture about one-third of the width of the whorl. It is orange-brown in color with a lighter area along the sutures. It measures about three-fourths of an inch in length.

This species occurs in the Hawaiian Islands and probably elsewhere in the Pacific area.

Lower Row, Right and Left

THE WASHED AUGER SHELL   *Terebra lauta* Pease

This auger shell is a rather small and uncommon species which is marked about the whorls by sharp-edged, longitudinal folds. It is of various colors but it is usually an orange brown color at the apex and becomes a lead gray color anteriorly. The shell is encircled toward the anterior end by a row of dark brownish spots placed just anterior to the sutures; the anterior end of the shell is tipped by the same brownish color. It is about one inch in length.

This species was described from the Hawaiian Islands and probably occurs elsewhere in the Pacific area.

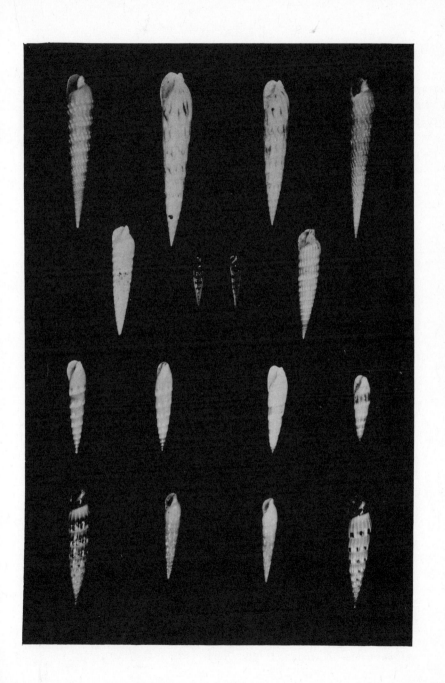

THE LITTLE PYRAMID SHELL FAMILY

FAMILY PYRAMIDELLIDAE

The molluscs of this family bear shells which are small, slender, conical or pyramidal shaped, and which consist of many whorls. In this family the columella is usually plicated with one or two folds, and the aperture is entire and is covered by a horny operculum. They are usually white in color and highly polished.

These molluscs are found on sandy bottoms in tropical and temperate seas.

Upper Row

THE LITTLE AUGER PYRAMID SHELL   *Pyramidella terebellum* (Müller)

This mollusc bears a shell which is smooth externally and thin in texture. The outer lip is simple and the columella bears two plicae. It is whitish or bluish in color and is marked by two spiral brownish bands upon the posterior whorls and by three or four brownish bands upon the body whorl. It will reach a length of about one inch.

This species is distributed from the Hawaiian Islands southward and westward through all of the islands of the tropical Pacific Ocean, through the East Indies, and across the Indian Ocean to Mauritius and the Red Sea.

Middle Row

THE FURROWED LITTLE PYRAMID SHELL   *Pyramidella sulcata* (A. Adams)

The shell of this mollusc is smooth on the outside and is marked by a spiral groove at the suture. The outer lip bears about five teeth within which may often be observed some distance back from the aperture. The columella bears three plications. This shell is white in color and is marked with longitudinal brownish blotches and often by spiral rows of brownish spots. It measures from one inch to one and one-half inches in length.

This mollusc is distributed from the Hawaiian Islands southward to Australia, westward across the entire tropical Pacific Ocean to the Philippine Islands, through the East Indies, and across the Indian Ocean to Mauritius and the Red Sea.

Lower Row

THE SWOLLEN PYRAMID SHELL   *Turbonilla varicosa* (A. Adams)

This is a slender frail species which is marked by longitudinal grooves and by wide longitudinal ribs which in turn bear spiral markings. The shell is constricted at the sutures giving the whorls an inflated appearance. The whorls are marked by varices which are usually white in color. The shell varies in color from a mottled white to a deep orange brown. It will reach a length of at least one inch.

This species is distributed from the Hawaiian Islands southward and westward into the tropical Pacific Ocean.

THE GREEN BUBBLE SHELL FAMILY

FAMILY HYDATINIDAE

The shells of these molluscs are oval in shape and very light and thin in texture. They have a body whorl which is very large, a low or nearly inconspicuous spire, and are usually marked with a beautiful pattern of colored stripes. The animal which inhabits the shell is large in size and possesses a gigantic foot. The head of the animal has a characteristic pair of folds developed from it which extend over a portion of the shell.

The green bubble shells make up a family of less than a dozen species which are found in the tropical Indo-Pacific and Atlantic Oceans.

Upper Row

THE BUBBLE SHELL   *Hydatina physis* (Linnaeus)

This mollusc bears a shell which is large and globular in outline, light and thin in texture, and which has depressed sutures and a thin, simple lip. The shell of this species is white in color and is covered over the outer surface with a thin, buff cuticle. This species may be distinguished by the dark wavy lines which encircle the shell. It will reach a length of about one and one-fourth inches.

This mollusc is distributed from the Hawaiian Islands southward and westward throughout Polynesia, along Australia, across the entire tropical Pacific Ocean to Japan, through the Philippine Islands and the Islands of the East Indies, and across the Indian Ocean to the coast of Africa and the Red Sea. It also occurs along the western shore of Africa and throughout the West Indies.

This species is one of the most widely distributed tropical forms in the world.

A slender, oval variety of this species with oblique brown lines has been called *Hydatina physis* (Linnaeus) variety *staminea* (Menke). Hawaiian specimens are regarded as belonging to this variety.

Middle and Lower Rows

THE SWOLLEN BUBBLE SHELL   *Hydatina (Aplustrum) amplustre* (Linn.)

This beautiful bubble shell is thin and smooth in texture and bears an aperture which is considerably enlarged at the anterior end. It is pink in color and is encircled by black and white bands. In life the shell is covered over the outer surface by a brown epidermis. It will reach at least one inch in length.

This species is distributed from the Hawaiian Islands southward to Australia, westward across the entire tropical Pacific Ocean, through the East Indies, and across the Indian Ocean to the coast of Africa.

THE GUAM BUBBLE SHELL   *Micromelo guamensis* (Quoy & Gaimard)

The Guam bubble shell is oval in shape and transparent in appearance. It is marked with three narrow equally spaced black spiral lines and by about ten black wavy longitudinal lines. It will reach about one-half inch in length.

This mollusc is distributed from the Hawaiian Islands southward and westward across the entire tropical Pacific Ocean, through the islands of the East Indies, and across the Indian Ocean to the coast of Africa.

Center

THE WHITE BANDED BUBBLE SHELL *Hydatina albocincta* (van der H.)

The shell of this mollusc is thin, smooth, and inflated. In life it is covered by a thin, transparent epidermis through which the color of the shell may be faintly seen. It is brownish in color and is marked with five wide white encircling bands. It will reach a length of nearly one and one-half inches.

This animal is distributed from the Hawaiian Islands southward and westward to Australia and thence across the entire tropical Pacific Ocean to Japan and the coast of China.

THE LINED BUBBLE-LIKE SHELL   *Bullina lineata* (Gray)

This mollusc has an oval shell of about four whorls; it bears a short spire and is covered by many fine encircling grooves. The aperture is quite large, although narrowed posteriorly, and the columella is nearly vertical and straight. It is white in color, often with a faint rosy tint, and is marked upon the outer surface by two very distinct spiral red lines and by numerous zigzag longitudinal reddish lines. It will reach a length of about one-half inch.

This mollusc is distributed from the Hawaiian Islands southward through Polynesia to New Zealand and Australia and westward across the tropical Pacific Ocean to Japan, through the East Indies, and across the Indian Ocean to the coast of Africa.

THE ACTAEON SHELL FAMILY

FAMILY ACTEONIDAE (PUPIDAE)

Within this family the shells are entirely external and are not buried in the flesh of the mollusc as they are in some related families. They are small in size, however, and are not capable of covering the entire animal when it is retracted into its shell. They are of spiral design and may bear a spire which is depressed or projecting and well developed. The surface of the shells within this family is usually marked with encircling punctured grooves. An operculum is always present.

This family was named for Actaeon, a hunter in ancient Greek mythology, who made the mistake of approaching the goddess Diana while she was bathing. As punishment for his error, Actaeon was changed by Diana into a stag whereupon his own hunting dogs set upon him and killed him.

THAANUM'S PUPPET SHELL   *Pupa thaanumi* Pilsbry

This species is a fairly solid shell, oval in outline, with a well developed, acute, conical spire; it is encircled by many fine grooves. The shell is whitish in color and is marked with irregular pinkish or reddish-brown spots which tend to form themselves into spiral rows. It will reach about one-half inch in length.

This species is known from the Hawaiian Islands and possibly elsewhere in the Pacific area. It is named for Mr. Ditlev Thaanum of Honolulu.

THE TRUE BUBBLE SHELL FAMILY
FAMILY BULLIDAE

The shells of these molluscs are egg shaped, thin and smooth in texture, and have a smooth lip bordering a large flaring aperture which is longer than the body whorl. These molluscs have large, fleshy, muscular bodies which enable them to burrow through the sand in search of other molluscs on which they feed. Most members of this family live in warm water.

Upper and Lower Rows

ADAMS' BUBBLE SHELL   *Bulla adamsi* (Menke)

This bubble shell is oval in shape and has a large and long aperture. This aperture is bordered by a lip which is nearly straight along its middle. Both the columellar and outer sides of the aperture have a white callous upon them. This shell is marbled and flecked with light and dark brown markings upon a somewhat tan background. It will reach a length of about one and one-half inches.

This species is distributed throughout Polynesia, along the tropical shores of Australia, and probably elsewhere in the Pacific area. It has been recently introduced into the Hawaiian Islands.

Center Row

PEASE'S BUBBLE SHELL   *Bulla peaseana* (Pilsbry)

Pease's bubble shell is quite oblong in shape and light and thin in texture. It is peculiar in having the edge of the outer lip straight for a considerable portion of its length. The surface of the shell is marked with fine longitudinal striae and with extremely fine spiral striae. It is mottled and flecked with various shades of brown and white. It will reach a length of about one inch.

This species is known from the Hawaiian Islands and possibly elsewhere in the Pacific area.

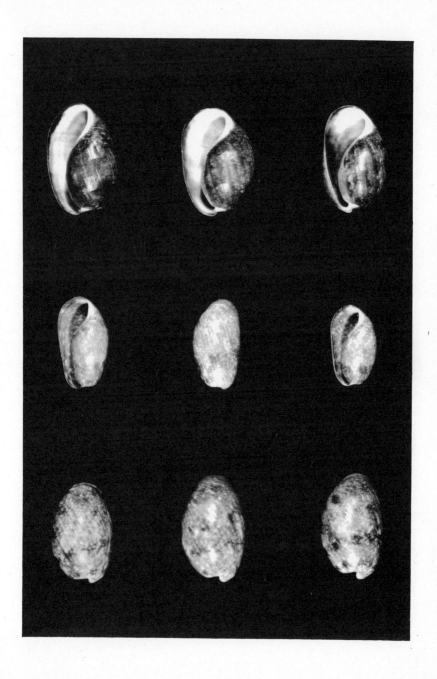

THE GLASSY BUBBLE SHELL FAMILY

Family Atyidae

Bubble shells are among the most frail and fragile of shells and are very difficult to collect without breaking. These shells are too small for the molluscs which inhabit them and are, as a consequence, nearly concealed by the animal which they are supposed to cover. These shells are oval or cylindrical in shape, are of very light, frail, thin texture, have a low or concealed spire, and are usually of a light brownish, or greenish color. They are found in muddy and brackish waters in warm, tropical seas.

Upper Row and Middle Row

THE SAFFRON YELLOW BUBBLE SHELL   *Haminoea crocata* Pease

This bubble shell is oval in shape and presents a shining surface which shows growth wrinkles and extremely fine spiral striations. It is of a transparent yellow or orange tint with opaque white at the extremities. It will reach a length of about one-half inch.

This species is found in the Hawaiian Islands and probably elsewhere in the tropical Pacific Ocean.

Lower Row

THE OPEN BUBBLE SHELL   *Haminoea aperta* Pease

The shell of this mollusc is oval in outline and somewhat swollen in the middle. It is smooth and thin in texture and is very finely longitudinally striate. It is of a whitish transparent color and will reach about one-half inch in length.

This species is found from the Hawaiian Islands southward throughout Polynesia and doubtless elsewhere in the tropical Pacific.

Some individuals regard the Hawaiian molluscs as a variety of the above species and know it under the name of *Haminoea aperta* Pease variety *oahuensis* Pilsbry.

THE HALF STRIPED CANOE SHELL   *Atys semistriata* Pease

This canoe shell has a thin, somewhat oval shell which is truncated at the ends and somewhat contracted posteriorly. It is marked by many spiral lines at both ends, but the middle of the shell is smooth. It is bluish white in color in the middle and opaque at the ends. It slightly exceeds one-half inch in length.

This mollusc is known from the Hawaiian Islands and probably elsewhere in the Pacific area.

THE SHORT CANOE SHELL   *Liloa curta* (A. Adams)

The shell of this mollusc is elongated and cylindrical in shape with truncated extremities and with a straight outer lip. The entire surface is spirally lined. It is thin in texture and of a semi-transparent white color. It will exceed one-half inch in length.

This mollusc is known from the Hawaiian Islands and probably extends from there to the Red Sea.

A narrower, more slender variety from the Hawaiian Islands has been called *Liloa curta* (A. Adams) variety *tomaculum* Pilsbry.

THE HORNED CANOE SHELL   *Atys cornuta* Pilsbry

The shell of this mollusc is cylindrical and oblong in shape and tapers at both ends. It is smooth in the middle and is marked with spiral lines at both ends. The posterior end bears a small tooth-like process. It is nearly white in color. It will reach a length of about one-half inch.

This species is known from the Hawaiian Islands.

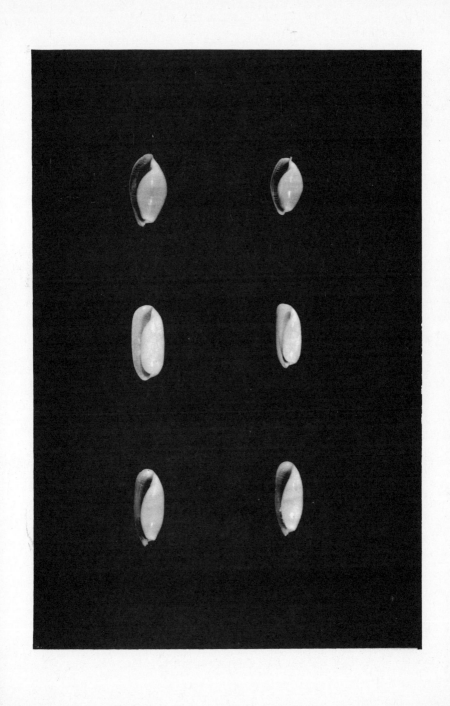

THE UMBRELLA SHELL FAMILY

FAMILY UMBRACULIDAE (UMBRELLIDAE)

The molluscs within this family are shaped somewhat like limpets, but, unlike the limpets, are not completely covered by their shell. They possess a large, thick, cylindrical shaped foot on the top of which rests a very thin, flattened and calcareous shell. The family is a small one and contains about six species.

THE CHINESE UMBRELLA SHELL   *Umbraculum sinicum* (Gmelin)

The Chinese umbrella shell is oval in outline and unusually thin for its size. It is of a very low conical shape with the apex situated behind and to the left of the center of the shell.

The color of this species is variable. In general the shell is white in color and is covered by a yellowish cuticle. The interior of the shell is usually darker than the exterior and is usually brown or orange-brown at the center. This central area is in turn surrounded by a yellowish band; it is encircled by a band of white along the outer margin. This shell will reach a length of nearly four inches.

The Chinese umbrella shell is distributed from the Hawaiian Islands southward and westward across the entire tropical Pacific Oean, through the islands of the East Indies, and across the Indian Ocean.

A form of the Chinese umbrella shell known as *U. sinicum* variety *aurantiacum* (Pease) is known from the Hawaiian Islands and possibly elsewhere in the Pacific area.

A more correct name for this shell is believed to be *Umbraculum umbraculum* (Humphrey).

THE EAR SHELL FAMILY

FAMILY ELLOBIIDAE

The ear shells have a spirally arranged shell which looks somewhat like the cone shells in general appearance. The outer surface of the shell is covered by a horny periostracum and the aperture is elongated and bears teeth or folds along its inner lip.

The ear shells are a family of more than one hundred species which are world wide in warm water.

Upper and Lower Rows

THE CHESTNUT COLORED EAR SHELL *Melampus castaneus* (Muhlfeld)

The chestnut colored ear shell is a small conical species with a short spire. It is a smooth polished shell and is covered in life by a smooth periostracum. The aperture of the shell is narrow and bears about seven teeth on the outer lip and about four on the inner lip. It will measure about one-half inch in length.

This species is distributed from the Hawaiian Islands southward and westward through the warm waters of the tropical Pacific Ocean.

Second Row

THE CLOSED EAR SHELL *Laemodonta clausa* (H. & A. Adams)

This little ear shell is comparatively thin and light in construction and bears an elevated conical spire. The outer surface is marked by encircling lines. The aperture is oval in outline and has three teeth or folds projecting into it from the inner lip and a single fold projecting into it from the outer lip. It is light brown in color, marked by darker brown areas and bands. Each whorl bears a dark central band and the anterior end of the shell is marked by a dark area. It is about one-fourth inch in length.

The specimens shown in the plate are from the Hawaiian Islands.

THE SIPHON SHELL FAMILY

FAMILY SIPHONARIIDAE

The siphon shells are often called false limpets because of their resemblance to the members of the limpet family. Like the limpets they are conical in shape and usually circular in outline at the base, but unlike the limpets they possess a radial groove on the inner side of the shell which makes a projection along the border of the base of the shell. These molluscs have gills together with a kind of a lung which permits them to live between the tides and to be out of the water for a great portion of the time. For this reason they have at times been considered as intermediate between aquatic and terrestrial forms of molluscs. In their normal habitat they are attached to rocks along the shoreline.

THE NORMAL SIPHON SHELL   *Siphonaria normalis* Gould

This siphon shell is shaped much like the limpets in general outline, form, and structure. It is a variable species marked upon the outer surface by radiating ridges of varying sizes. The interior of the shell is smooth and polished although it may be uneven and show evidences of its radial sculpture, particularly at the margins of the shell. It is variously colored, but is usually brownish or bluish without, and is often nearly white upon the ridges. The interior of the shell is also variously colored, but is usually of a brownish or bluish hue. It is usually darkest near the apex with a light blue area along the margin; it is marked by short radial lines, extending inward from the margin. It ranges from one-fourth to nearly one inch in length.

The siphon shells are a puzzling group and the naming of them is accompanied by considerable difficulty and uncertainty. It is with some hesitation that names are offered for the species pictured here. Some individuals regard this species as a variable one while other prefer to further designate it. The name of *Siphonaria normalis* Gould variety *omaria* Reeve is offered for those shells which are smaller in size and in which the ribs and other details are smaller, finer, and more delicate in sculpture. The name of *Siphonaria normalis* Gould variety *chirura* Pilsbry is often applied to the form in which the ribs are very heavy and extend beyond the margin of the shell.

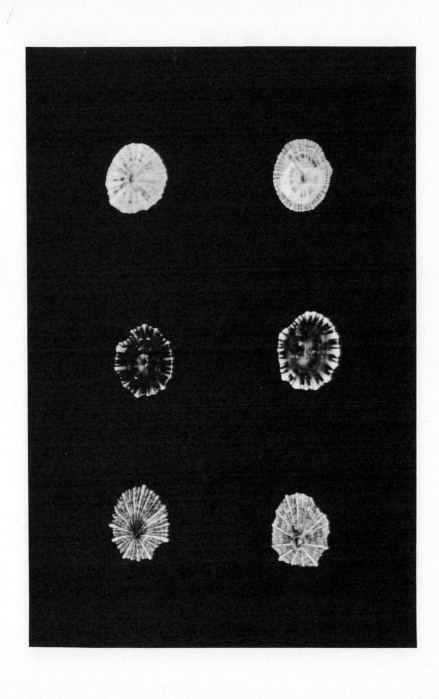

THE CHITONS
CLASS AMPHINEURA

The chitons compose one of the five great groups of molluscs. They are animals which are bilaterally symmetrical in form, dorso-ventrally flattened, and bear a series of eight transverse plates in a longitudinal row down their backs. These plates, which overlap much like the shingles of a house, are bordered by an encircling band of muscle called the girdle. The lower side of the body usually bears a large foot upon which the animal creeps. Gills lie between this foot and the mantle.

Chitons are divided into two large groups. One group, the Polyplacophora (with plates), includes those chitons which possess the series of eight over-lapping plates upon their upper surface and have the head marked off from the body. In this group the sexes are separate and the gills are numerous and are placed upon each side of the body between the foot and the mantle. The second group, known as the Aplacophora (without plates), have bodies which are more worm-like in shape and appearance. The conspicuous plates, so characteristic of the other chitons, are missing and the broad foot is much reduced in size.

The chitons are all slow moving marine molluscs which are widely distributed through all oceans. They subsist upon vegetation.

THE PRICKLY OR THORNY CHITON FAMILY
FAMILY ACANTHOCHITONIDAE

The chitons of this family take their name from the fact that many members of the group bear tufts of hair in the girdle which encircles the body. The eight plates upon the upper surface of the body are more completely covered upon their outer margin by the girdle than in other families of this group.

THE GREENISH THORNY CHITON   *Acanthochiton viridis* Pease

In common with the other members of this family, this chiton possesses the broad foot, the eight plates, the encircling girdle, and the tufts of bristles around the body. The plates are semilunar in shape, smooth in the middle, granulated upon the sides, and of a light blue color. The animal as a whole is of a greenish color and is often marked with a white or light colored line down the middle of the body. The tufts of bristles are of a darker green color than the body of the animal.

This chiton is known from the Hawaiian Islands and possibly elsewhere in the Pacific area.

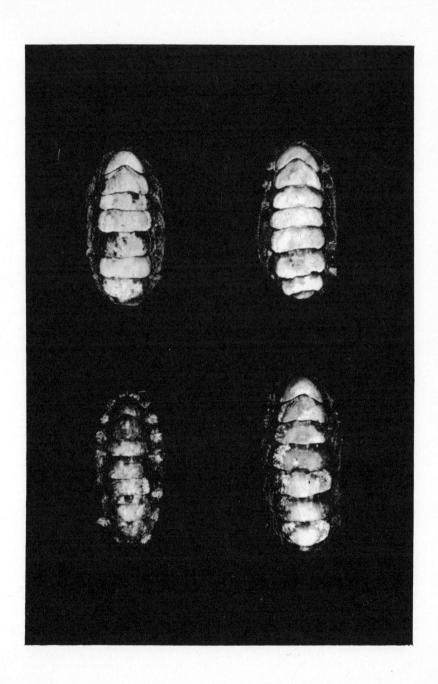

THE TOOTH SHELLS OR ELEPHANT TUSK SHELLS

CLASS SCAPHOPODA

The tooth shells are one of the five large groups or classes of molluscs and receive their common name from the fact that their shells are somewhat like the tusks or teeth of elephants. Like the elephant's tusk these shells are long, curved, tapering, and hollow; but, unlike the teeth of other animals, these shells are open at both ends. Within this tubular shell is a tubular mantle which secretes the shell and which encloses the body except at the open ends of the shell. The larger end of the shell is the anterior end and contains a rudimentary head, a muscular foot for burrowing in the sand, and some filaments which seem to serve as sense organs and help in the capture of food. The heart and the eyes are absent in these molluscs and, although the head is small and rudimentary, it bears the characteristic radula.

In life the head end of these animals lies buried in the sand while the smaller posterior end projects above the surface. It is through this smaller posterior end of the shell that water is drawn into and passes out of the mantle cavity. The gills found in most other molluscs are lacking in these forms so that the duties of respiration are performed by the mantle.

Tooth shells are all marine molluscs and make their home on the bottom of the ocean from the shoreline down to considerable depths. They seem to prefer to make their home in areas which are sandy and free from organic materials.

The tooth shells are a small group of molluscs and, in spite of the fact that there are very few kinds, are a difficult group to classify.

The species figured in the accompanying plate is a member of the genus *Dentalium* dredged off the Hawaiian Islands.

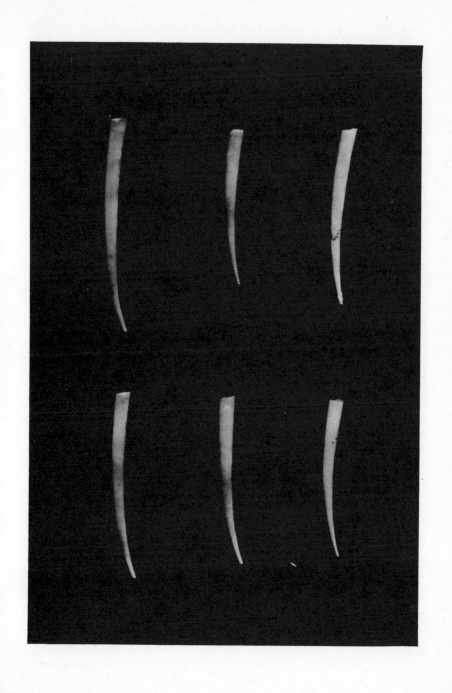

THE CEPHALOPODS

Class Cephalopoda

The cephalopods are divided into two groups or orders, the Dibranchiata and the Tetrabranchiata.

The Dibranchiata have two gills, horny jaws, eight or ten arms, and usually no shell or, if any, an internal one. This group is further divided into the Octopoda (eight arms) and the Decapoda (ten arms). The Octopoda include the octopods and the argonauts; the Decapoda include the squids and the small *Spirula*.

The Tetrabranchiata have four gills, shelly jaws, many more arms without suckers, and an external shell. This group incudes the nautiloids.

THE ARGONAUT FAMILY

Family Argonautidae

The argonauts possess no shell and are free swimming creatures which live in the open sea. The "paper nautilus" of shell collectors is not the shell of a nautilus, but in reality the egg case of the female argonaut and is formed by secretion from the expanded web-like ends of the upper pair of arms of the female.

Prior to mating, the sperm of the male is stored within the third arm on the left side. This arm becomes detached (hectocotylized) during mating and is thereafter found in the mantle cavity of the female. The male argonaut, which is much smaller than the female, is reported to be less than one inch in length.

This family is the group mentioned in the writings of the ancients as the Nautilus. There are about three present day species.

The Paper Nautilus   *Argonauta argo* Linnaeus

The egg case or "shell" of the argonaut is very light, thin, and frail in construction. It is flattened in shape and is covered over the sides of the exterior by radiating ribs which divide as they proceed from the center. The keels of the shell are marked by a row of numerous, small, fairly sharp tubercles. It is white with brown markings upon the keel and measures from six to ten inches in diameter.

This species is world wide in warm water. It occurs in the Pacific, Indian, and Atlantic Oceans, in the Mediterranean Sea, and in the Gulf of California.

THE SPIRULA FAMILY

FAMILY SPIRULIDAE

This family belongs in the decapod group of the two gilled cephalopods. They are animals with an elongated body and look much like a small squid. They are covered over the posterior part of the body with a small shell which is loosely coiled in one plane and which is chambered within, somewhat like the Nautilus. This shell is held upright at the end of the body by the mantle and is almost completely enclosed within it.

THE POINTED SPIRULA   *Spirula peronii* Lamarck

The shell of this mollusc is of the usual cylindrical or conical tapering form with the coils lying in one plane and with each chamber separated from the last by a partition or septum which is concave in shape toward the open end and which is connected to the preceeding septum and chamber by a ventrally located funnel shaped siphonal tube. The last chamber of the shell is the largest, while the first or nuclear chamber of the shell is rounded or bulbous. The shell is white in color. It will reach about three-fourths of an inch in diameter.

This species inhabits the tropical Atlantic and Pacific Oceans. It is probably world wide in the warmer oceans of the globe.

THE NAUTILUS FAMILY

FAMILY NAUTILIDAE

The nautiloids belong to the group of the cephalopods which have four gills. They were once a large and important group in the seas of ancient times, but today only a few species remain. Although the group includes animals with both straight and coiled shells, only those with coiled shells remain today, the others having perished in ancient times. The shells of these molluscs are of a conical, spiral design and are coiled upon a single plane. They are smooth externally, or very nearly so, and have the interior of the shell divided into a series of chambers by single, simple, curved septa of which the last chamber is the largest. The animal lives in the last chamber or open end of the shell and builds new and larger chambers as it continues to grow. The various species inhabit the open ocean of all tropical seas.

This family contains but a single genus. There are at least six living species and more than six hundred species of fossils.

THE PEARLY OR CHAMBERED NAUTILUS   *Nautilus pompilius* Lamarck

The shell of this nautilus is nearly circular in design with a smooth exterior and interior and with the umbilicus covered by a callous deposit. It is white or whitish in color and is marked in a radial fashion by red or red-brown.

This species is known from Polynesia and the waters of the tropical Pacific Ocean.

INDEX